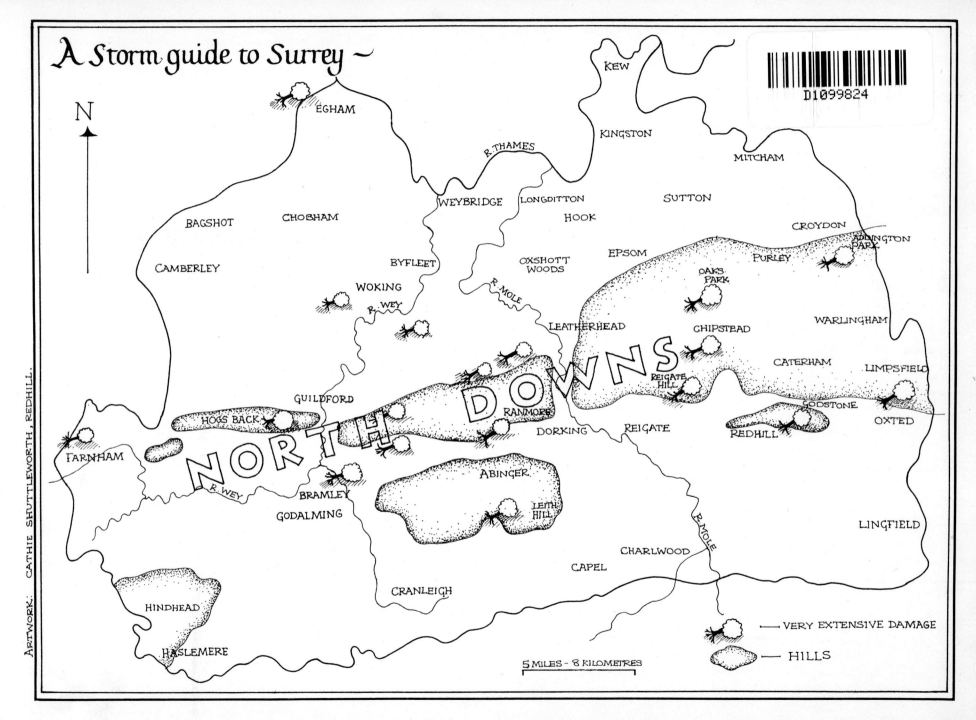

A Storm guide to Surrey ~

N

KEW

EGHAM

KINGSTON

R. THAMES

MITCHAM

WEYBRIDGE   LONGDITTON   SUTTON

BAGSHOT   CHOBHAM   HOOK   CROYDON

ADDINGTON PARK

CAMBERLEY   BYFLEET   OXSHOTT WOODS   EPSOM   PURLEY

OAKS PARK

WOKING   R. MOLE   WARLINGHAM

R. WEY   LEATHERHEAD   CHIPSTEAD

CATERHAM   LIMPSFIELD

NORTH DOWNS

REIGATE HILL

GUILDFORD   RANMORE   GODSTONE

HOGS BACK   DORKING   REIGATE   REDHILL   OXTED

FARNHAM

R. WEY   BRAMLEY   ABINGER

GODALMING   LEITH HILL   LINGFIELD

R. MOLE

CHARLWOOD

CAPEL

CRANLEIGH

HINDHEAD

HASLEMERE

— VERY EXTENSIVE DAMAGE

5 MILES - 8 KILOMETRES   — HILLS

ARTWORK: CATHIE SHUTTLEWORTH, REDHILL.

1

Surrey Wildlife Trust

Part of the proceeds from the sale of this book will be donated to The Surrey Wildlife Trust and other county woodland appeals.

Published by Froglets Publications Ltd, Brasted Chart, Westerham 0959 62972.

© Froglets, 1988

ISBN 0-9513019-2-0

This book was fully produced by
Pen & Ink Publicity Services,
9 Cannon Lane, Tonbridge, Kent TN9 1PP.

*Front cover photograph:
The sheer force of nature at Woodside Green, Croydon by Brian Waite.*

*Back cover photograph:
After the Storm. Woodland on the former Shabden Park, Estate,
by Ian Moorhouse.*

The preparation of this book would not have been possible without the co-operation of the following.

Meteorological Office, Bracknell
Surrey Mirror and Sutton Herald Series
Surrey County Council
Croydon Advertiser
University of Dundee
Farnham Library
Dorking and Leatherhead Advertisers
Surrey Comet
Camberley and Yateley News and Mail
Esher News
Woking News
Croydon Council Parks Department
— Mr Bill Gilmore
Croydon Council Building Services
Croydon Library Service
Sutton Library and Council
Residents of Bankside Close
Oaks Park staff and head park keeper
Mr Pearson
London Weather Centre
Climatological Observers Link
Met Office, Gatwick
Redhill 101 Club
Royal Botanical Gardens,
Kew and J. Keesing
Paul Adams, Long Ditton
Croydon Council Highways department
Surrey Advertiser Pippa Faux
Mr K. C. Ollier, Croydon Council
Royal Meteorological Society
The Moorhouse family, Reeves Rest
Jenny Currie
Mr K. Hustwick, Camberley
Mr T. Hughes, Warlingham
Grinstead Butchers, Bramley
Mrs Mary Bryant
Mr Graham Larcombe
Mr John Elms

Gordon Allis, N. McGinn, J. Stuart,
K. Walter, R. Heron, M. Case-Green
Norman Hurricane Smith
Wallington white watch fire crew
Bob Jackson
Dauncey family
N and M. Davison
Warden, Painshill Park
John Powell
Waverley Council
Croydon Natural History & Scientific Society
Runnymede Council
Kingston Council
Woking Council
Spelthorne Council
David Tippet-Wilson
M. Beardall
Haslemere Herald
Barbara Edwards
Ann Cattermole
Surrey Herald
Egham News
Staines and Ashford Leader
David Scorer
Bob Jackson
Seeboard, Guildford
Linda Brockey
BT Croydon
Headley Tea Rooms
Greta Morley,
Adam Forde
Lewis Smith
Barbara McDonald, Camberley News
Amanda Whittington, Aldershot News
A. J. Russell, Farnham
Fern Flynn
St Paul's Church, Hook
Peter Butler, Hook

This book is dedicated to the men and women of the emergency services throughout the county of Surrey. They responded to a crisis with courage and efficiency.

Surrey in The Hurricane

by Mark Davison and Ian Currie

The wind that blew in from the sea in the early hours of October 16, 1987 and changed the face of southern England prompted newspaper editor, Bob Ogley, to produce a book that has become almost as famous as the storm itself. *In The Wake of The Hurricane*, published by Froglets Publications, was an instant best-seller and in demand all over the world. It also raised more than £30,000 for woodland and garden appeals. This sister book, researched and written by Mark Davison and Ian Currie, shows how the great tree county of Surrey stood squarely in the path of the most frightening storm ever known and suffered terrible devastation. It also shows how Surrey is patching up its many wounds and replanting carefully and lovingly for the future.

Introduction

by Bob Ogley

THE county of Surrey has often been described as London's doorstep, a county of commuters whose lives are expended elsewhere and a county invaded by cheerful hordes on a day's outing from the drabness of suburbia. When the weather is at its best, intrusion is at its worst.

Surrey, however, has much more to offer. It may be one of the smallest counties in England but it is also one of the most beautiful. There are vast areas of wide open countryside, attractive villages, towns and great houses like Polesden Lacey, Clandon Park, Sutton Place and Loseley. Other natural beauties include the North Downs, Leith Hill, the Devil's Punchbowl, Frensham Ponds, Epsom Downs, the Hogs Back and three rivers, the great Thames itself and those responsible for the greenness of the county, the Mole and the Wey.

It is those who live in Surrey who know it as it really is; a tree county where gently sweeping wooded hillsides reach great heights and provide an escape route from the invaders below. Leith Hill, 965 feet, Holmbury, 857, Hindhead, 895, are among the highest and the most wooded peaks in southern England.

Surrey is also renowned for its individual trees. A cedar of Lebanon at Pains Hill, Cobham, is supposed to be the biggest in England; at Addlestone is the well-known Crouch Oak, 24 feet round; the yew at Crowhurst has a girth of 11 yards and room for a dozen people to sit at a table. There are grand old yews at Tandridge, Mickleham and Hambledon and the oldest tulip tree in England is still living in the grounds of Esher Place.

The great storm drastically altered the Surrey woodlands, opened up great wide vistas and felled many of its famous trees. It also brought a heightened awareness of the need for careful management of the woodlands for future generations to enjoy. The Surrey Wildlife Trust has initiated a county-wide woodlands survey and a stalwart band of volunteers has been co-ordinated to research more than 1,000 sample areas.

This book is a pictorial record of a county renowned for its woodlands and gardens which was devastated by winds gusting at more than 100 miles an hour. But it also shows the beneficial effects; how clearings and fallen timber enhance the wildlife value of woodlands and how replanting is taking place with such loving care.

Like other areas of southern England, October 16, 1987 was the county's date with history. Surrey in the Hurricane became folklore on the very morning of that memorable day.

Contents

I'm wild about Surrey

by David Bellamy, B.Sc. Ph D, FLS

CLOSE your eyes and think about the county of Surrey. What does your mind perceive? The stockbroker belt, perhaps. Fashionable, elegant homes. Fast trains and the first class ticket holder. Motorways. Tourists. The Oval. Cricket on the village green. Good neighbours. Wentworth. Epsom Downs. Hacking and hunting. Trim towns . . . .

Not many, I bet, think about the real quality of life up there on the hills and downs where the woodlands provide an antidote to a day in the city. The perfect sanctuary.

I think about it but then I was born in Surrey, went to school at Sutton and, by profession, I'm a botanist. In the meantime I've travelled to paradise and back but still feel happy in this great tree county. I love the beauty of the landscape and its woodlands. For myriads of wild plants and animals it's home. It's also my grass roots home.

When the trees fell down, a new feeling of patriotism surged through Surrey hearts. Good neighbours looked at each other, then looked at the woodlands in shock horror. Their heritage had gone. The work of some of the greatest landscape artists lay askew across their county.

Let's mourn, but not moan. Like a dose of salts the storm had wonderful beneficial effects, enhancing diversity and wildlife value, stimulating new growth and a new awareness that the landscape does not stand still. It needs constant, careful management.

I am privileged to be a founder member and President of the Surrey Wildlife Trust. I am also part of the management team and know this book is supporting that cause. Liz Brown, our "storm officer" has been doing sterling work in encouraging landowners to restrict clearance to a minimum. She and her volunteers are also surveying the woods; they will help replant carefully and lovingly and also allow nature to regenerate.

This book by Mark and Ian must not be seen as a disaster book, but a book of new opportunity. The pictures are dramatic and the stories of courage shine like sunlight through those gaps which nature's power has punched in the hillsides. When you finally put it down you will see that the future is, indeed, bright.

Close your eyes and think of Surrey. It's a fabulous place, isn't it? Join the Trust and help keep it that way.

Planting for the future. David Bellamy with his younger friends.

5

The Rev Harry Forder outside his shattered house.

One more miracle

THE Rev Harry Forder of Grove Cottage, Levylsdene, near Guildford will never know how he survived the night of October 16, 1987 when a tree fell on his house and sent him crashing through the floor to the hall below. This is Mr Forder's story in his own words.

❛Three weeks after my wife and I had retired from our parish of St Mary's, West Horsley and settled in our new house at Merrow the hurricane caused an enormous beech tree to crash on to the house. The noise before it happened was just like aeroplane engines roaring before an air raid during the war. I expected something to happen — and it did!

Suddenly, the attic collapsed on top of us, dropping a beam across my wife while I was hurled down to the ground floor, incredibly landing in the hall next to the telephone which worked just long enough for me to dial '999'. After I made the call the line went dead. Beams and rubble were falling around me. I knew my wife was upstairs but did not know if she was all right. But I do know that the roof was falling around her and her legs were trapped by beams. She was trying to feel round in the darkness for something to put over her head to protect herself. She called out to me and was relieved when I called back. Then we both heard, with joy, our dog George (a bearded collie 14 years old) bark.

Not long after, the fire engine and ambulance arrived, which was a miracle in itself as trees were falling across the roads every few yards. Firemen rescued my wife and George by ladder and we were all unharmed.

Since the October experience we lived in rented accommodation until returning to a newly-built house where the stump of the offending tree will be a constant reminder to that terrible night.❜

After his experience the Rev Forder told reporters that he wasn't lucky. "You make your own luck,' he said. 'This was a miracle.'

Photograph: Surrey Herald

When the fire services arrived to rescue the occupants of these houses in Addlestone, their floodlights revealed the extent of the damage. Half of one bedroom had disappeared and the front of the house had been knocked about two inches sideways leaving an ugly diagonal crack. The roof was severely damaged and the chimney had fallen into next door's garage. The other trunk of the cedar embedded itself into the roof. Two garages were demolished and five cars completely squashed. This was Surrey on the night of the storm.

An Exceptionally Strong Pressure Gradient Over Southern England

LOW
958
mbs
108 mph
surrey
99 mph
104 mph
104 mph
104 mph
115 mph
962mbs
978mbs
970mbs
16 Oct 87
0400 hrs

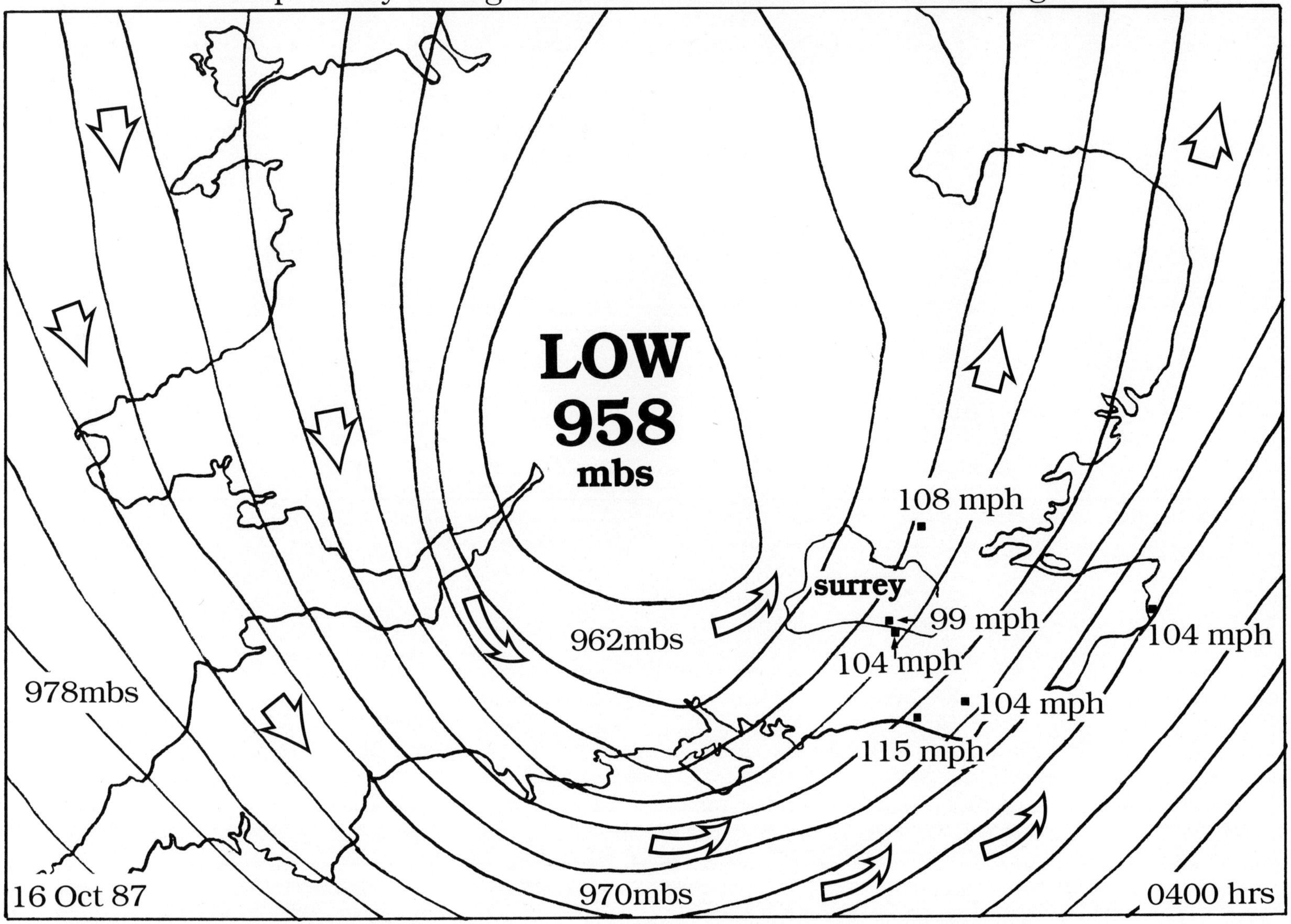

The isobar map which shows lines of equal barometric pressure, indicates unprecedented gradients over Southern England at 4am when the storm was raging. The lines are very similar to contours drawn on a map. The closer together they are, the steeper the slope. Normally there would be only two or three pressure lines, since they are drawn at two millibar intervals. Between London and the South East coast there was an amazing difference of 12 millibars. On a map like this, these lines are a good pointer to wind strengths. The wind speed exceeded 100 mph over a wide area, with the most damage being recorded to the south and east of the low pressure centre. This area of low pressure reached 952 mbs a few hours earlier and was the deepest October low this century. As it moved away north-east, there was a record rise of pressure.

Meteorological Account

AROUND mid-evening on Thursday October 15 1987 anyone out walking their dog after a day of rain or merely putting out an empty milk bottle may have felt an unusual warmth to the air, but gave it little thought. The wind blew gently, a soft whispering in the trees. For those with barometers in the hallway there may have been a second glance as the glass showed the pressure was low and still falling. Most people went to bed peacefully and blissfully unaware that away to the south-west, gathering its forces over Biscay, was a tempest that in a few frenetic hours before dawn, would unleash its pent-up fury on virtually every community in Surrey and change the face of our woodlands for generations to come.

It had been a very wet October prior to the storm. Active weather fronts had crossed Surrey, and by the 15th over six inches (150mm) had fallen at Coulsdon. This was twice the average for the whole month. The upper air winds of the jet stream, the steering and controlling force of the movement of depressions and their associated weather fronts, were much further south than was usual for this time of year. In Biscay, sea temperatures were warmer than normal and off the Florida coast on October 13 air from hurricane Floyd flowed north-eastwards into the jet stream. Here was the possible trigger for the sudden development and explosive deepening of the depression that was to become a vicious storm.

A satellite photograph taken at 2.47pm on the 15th shows an area of strongly rising air ahead of a polar vortex. The contrast between the warm air mass to the east of the vortex and that of the polar air is becoming more extreme. The warmth of the air ahead of the storm can be shown by midnight values of 17°C (63°F) and 18°C (64°F) over East Surrey and Kent not far off from the all-time record day maximum temperatures for the time of the year. There were unprecedented rises of temperatures exceeding 9°C in 20 minutes to the north-west of London. As the storm centre made landfall close to Exeter, pressure values were at their lowest in October for at least 150 years. By 03.00 hours on the 16th the full force of the storm was being felt across southern England.

There was an exceptionally strong pressure gradient over Surrey as the 04.00 hours GMT chart shows.

The closer together the isobar spacing the stronger the winds. As the storm moved north-east over the Midlands the gradient became tighter over Surrey. The London Weather Centre reported a gust of wind of 82 knots (94 mph) at 2.50am, a record there by a wide margin, while the British Telecom Tower recorded 94 knots (108 mph) before the anemometer broke. At Gatwick a gust of 86 knots (99 mph) at 04.30 hours was also a record and closed the airport, while on another Gatwick instrument, 90 knots (104 mph) was observed. Heathrow's 80 knots (92 mph) smashed the 1959 record by 28 knots.

Winds were even stronger on the coast. At Shoreham-by-Sea a speed of 100 knots (115 mph) at 03.30 hours was recorded and three hours earlier at the Points du Roc on the Normandy Coast an even greater speed of 117 knots (135 mph) was recorded. Such winds brought salt spray far inland across Surrey and windows and cars in Croydon were in urgent need of cleaning once other more important tasks in the big clear-up were complete.

As the storm continued to move north-east there were record rises of pressure with more than 23 millibars in three hours, estimated as having a return period of 200 years.

The storm was over but it left behind scenes of utter devastation, none more so than in woodlands. Trees were still in leaf, the soil was waterlogged and the wind had come in great gusts. These factors were largely responsible for the estimated felling of 15 million trees in southern and eastern England. Aerial photographs have revealed areas with as much as an 80 per cent loss of their woodland with swathes of destruction parallel to the wind direction. Damage along valleys and on lee slopes suggests topographically enhanced acceleration of the wind to values well beyond those at known recording sites, and breaks in the path of damage suggest a very turbulent flow. Oaks Park near Sutton is a good example of these aspects of the storm where shallow-rooted beech trees were the major casualty, especially those positioned alongside a shallow north-south inclined valley on the dip slope of the North Downs.

The storm in the early hours of Friday 16th was the most severe since the famous Defoe storm of 1703. With one in six householders in the South East submitting an insurance claim and with the insured cost totalling £1500 million, it was by far the most costly in financial terms. The tragedy was that 19 people lost their lives in the storm, but the timing meant that this total was small compared to the catastrophe that might have been if the storm had struck during daylight hours.

Photograph: Sutton Council Leisure Services.

Barely one in five trees remain in this area of Oaks Park, near Banstead. Wallington's fire crew were trapped here at the height of the storm.

A peaceful scene but many tell-tale signs in Grange Park, Beddington by the River Wandle.

Guildford and Cranleigh

AS the storm approached from the south-west, Guildford was one of Surrey's first large towns to suffer the searing wind which hit the city like a whirlwind. So ferocious were the gusts that 16 metal garage doors, lashed down at Guildford Borough Council's depot, took off like flying saucers. One came to rest at a garden at Stoke Lock and many were retrieved from around the depot area. A week later four doors had still not been found.

Guildford is an important centre that attracts many visitors. It is proud of its historical and architectural heritage; its busy and contemporary shopping precincts. On Friday morning October 16 there were neither tourists nor shoppers — just damaged buildings, leaning trees, tons of debris and an uncanny, almost eerie silence.

Those who lived close to the town centre would not have been aware that this was the worst storm to hit Surrey for 284 years and that the downs on either side of the road between Guildford and Cranleigh were a twisted and tangled heap of flailing limbs, reaching almost helplessly towards the sky. They did not know how many homes had been hit by falling trees and of all those miraculous escapes which provided neighbours with a talking point for many months to come.

This was a feature of the storm as a physiotherapist at the town's St Luke's Hospital and her husband know only too well. The couple climbed out of bed just minutes before their ceiling collapsed. They would have been buried alive.

The nerve centre of a massive rescue operation was set up at Guildford Borough Council where an emergency team gave priority to the old. Meals on Wheels organisers were alerted and they prepared scores of extra lunches for old people's homes at Ash, Albury and Worplesdon which had been plunged into darkness. Bottle gas heaters were rushed to private nursing homes and then to the Borough's own tenants.

Almost 200 emergency calls were made to the council in the three days after the storm. Many concerned the dangerous state of the woods, particularly at Newlands Corner, Whitmore Common and St Martin's Hill. Surrey County Council warned the people of Guildford and district to stay away from these areas.

An indication of the material damage caused by the storm lay in the number of calls for urgent roof repairs. In the following week 479 emergency repairs were carried out to council homes and in the private sector negotiations with insurance companies continued for many months.

One more immediate worry for the Borough concerned the number of hazardous trees on the 2,600 acres it administers and it was necessary to write £70,000 in the 88/89 budget to cover the clearing up bill. It was the most expensive and the longest emergency Guildford had ever known.

No sooner had the storm abated, than there was a new hazard along the river valley in the form of floods. The whole stretch of the Wey Navigation from Weybridge to Godalming was closed to the public and many farms and homes were flooded. As the days passed the debris from fallen trees helped the river to swell even further.

The face of Guildford, Cranleigh and their wooded downs today is so different. Huge gaps have been punched into the landscape and this new combination of light and space is not always welcome although the lost trees are being replaced with the same species.

Priceless Lebanese cedars dating back to the early 1600's were blown over in Peper Harow Park, near Elstead. The cedars were some of the first to be introduced into this country and seeds from them were later sent to Kew Gardens for germination. In the neighbouring village of Elstead, locals opened up the United Reformed Church to offer hot meals to those without power. A car with loudhailer toured the village advertising the service.

When the flak flew

By former BBC weather
forecaster Barbara Edwards

I slept through the worst of the storm, and felt quite cheated at missing the meteorological event of the century. From a meteorologist's point of view, really bad weather is so much more interesting and exciting than good weather!

When we were eventually woken at about six o'clock by the noise of the wind and a loose tile flapping on the roof above our heads, my husband's first reaction was: "They didn't forecast this". As usual I immediately sprang to 'their' defence, explaining that "Bill (Giles) did have 50 mile an hour winds down the North Sea on last night's chart —they probably just moved a bit further inland." Little did I realise at the time that winds over most of south-east England were well in excess of 50 mph and my husband's remark was nearer the truth.

The reality of the situation began to dawn when we discovered there was no radio, no television, and the 'phone, while not entirely dead, just made strange noises. My husband, who commutes to the City, set off for Egham station, only to return shortly with the tale of roads blocked and no trains. Obviously nobody was going anywhere that morning.

As Aunty Beeb staggered into life in fits and starts and we began to hear the incredible stories of events of that night, we realised how lucky we had been. While surrounded by damage and devastation, a quick reconnaissance of our house and garden showed we had escaped virtually unscathed.

Towards midday, as the winds gradually abated and roads were cleared, we ventured into Egham town and were surprised to see a westbound train in the station. We were told it had been there since 3 am and the passengers were completely stranded, not being able to continue their journey either by road or rail. There being no catering facilities at the station, a member of British Rail staff had been sent out to purchase food and drink to sustain the passengers in their ordeal. I often wonder what happened to those people and how much longer their unscheduled stop lasted.

We went on to Englefield Green, a nearby village on top of a hill overlooking Runnymede and Windsor. Being that much higher and more exposed to the wind, the damage here was even worse, great numbers of trees being ripped out of the ground and tossed aside like matchsticks, often leaving holes in the ground like bomb craters.

I was overawed by the sheer power that had been generated to do this, and when people ask if man will ever be able to control the weather the answer must surely be no. How could one harness power like that?

Being keen golfers and living only about two miles from Wentworth, we were appalled to see the damage to that lovely course. At our own club at nearby Ashford it was a similar story. The entrance was completely blocked, and one of the larger trees had fractured a gas main, so the steward and his wife were marooned with no way out and no cooking facilities.

One felled chestnut tree housed a bees' nest in its trunk but the bees seemed unmoved by their home being rotated through 90° from the vertical to the horizontal and stayed there throughout the winter. The old mulberry tree by the eighth green was still standing, although with a noticeable list which was not there before.

Having watched numerous news and weather broadcasts throughout that day I began to feel very sorry for my ex-colleagues at the Met. Office; Bill, Mike (Fish) and Ian, (McGaskill) as they came under increasing flak from the press and media. As the front men, they were getting all the blame and criticism, while the people who actually dictate what the forecast is to be, remained anonymously in the background.

Another depression

BBC weatherman Michael Fish visited storm-torn Surrey when he spoke to a meeting of the Surrey Federation of Women's Institutes at Dorking Halls. It was only ten days after the gale and Mr Fish was still under the weather over all the adverse publicity in the country's tabloid papers.

Mrs Elizabeth Southey, introduced Mr Fish to his audience. She appealed to the ladies 'to be kind'. Mr Fish was asked by one lady what had happened to the woman who had telephoned the BBC asking if there was a hurricane on the way, and was assured that there was no need to worry, there won't be a hurricane.

Mr Fish attacked the tabloid papers and said the woman was talking about 'an entirely different depression.' He hoped this statement would be splashed across the headlines.

On the day after the storm, Mr Fish, and the Director General of the Meteorological Office, Mr J. T. Houghton were besieged by reporters and cameramen, seeking answers as to why there had been no warning of the storm.

Photograph: D. N. Boucher

Before the Great Storm changed the landscape of Surrey, Wray Lane at Reigate Hill was a serene, sunlit avenue of trees leading from the Holmesdale Valley to the North Downs Way.

14

This was the same area of Wray Lane after the storm left the leafy lane virtually tree-less, huge chalky root-balls blocked every path in view.

A massive root ball towering almost two storeys high dominates the foreground. As the signpost says there was beech all over the lawn of this Guildford house just two streets from St Luke's Hospital.

Photograph: Surrey Advertiser

Thousands of visitors flock to Clandon Park near Guildford every year. One of the attractions was a graceful avenue of beech trees leading to the Palladian-style house. In the furious storm, most of these specimens toppled like nine pins and the whole skyline changed overnight. It was the second blow to befall the estate — for eight beeches fell in storm force winds the previous spring.

17

The dead and wounded in Addington Park lay in state for many months after the storm. The loss of this Croydon wood near Gravel Hill was particularly mourned.

The Royal Horticultural Society's garden at Wisley suffered with the rest. Here we see the beheaded blue spruce Picea Pungens Glauca.

A spectacular collapse. This is the Wey Valley Bowls Club near Guildford.

Photograph: Surrey Advertiser

Photographs: Surrey Advertiser

Shalford, a village between Guildford and Albury, had a landmark before the storm. It was a gracious blue cedar which stood proudly outside the parish church of St Mary. The roots were prised from the ground and the rustic seat and concrete plinth upturned.

In the village of Compton, south west of Guildford, a large cedar in the grounds of a neighbouring manor house narrowly missed the ancient St Nicholas Church. Further up the road in the Elizabethan Loseley House, the woods were devastated. There a crane was brought in to help save the historic Mulberry tree planted by Queen Mary, wife of King George V, in 1933.

The church and nearby cottages at Alfold in the Wealden Forest, were struck by falling pines. The 40 foot high spruce (above) fell on Mr and Mrs Donald Walker's period home, and the church itself suffered thousands of pounds worth of damage to parts of its 11th century structure.

Adjacent to South Croydon recreation ground the huge plane had no mercy for the old Austin.

The chapel at Hazelwood Preparatory School Limpsfield was a casualty together with some classrooms.

Martin Lockyer of Gadbridge Lane, Ewhurst, looks ruefully at his two day old, £14,000 Rover. It was a write off. Heavily wooded areas of Surrey suffered badly and Forest Green and Walliswood nearby were among the last villages in the county to have their power restored.

Photograph: Surrey Advertiser

Residents of Gadbridge Lane, Ewhurst, team up to clear hundreds of blocked roads in and around their delightful village. Pitch Hill, which lies to the north west of Ewhurst and rises to 843 feet above sea level was devastated by the storm. The reservoir at Hurtwood was damaged by falling trees and residents in Abinger Hammer, Holmbury St Mary and Coldharbour were without water for many days.

Photograph: Surrey Advertiser

Woods on the south facing slopes of the Surrey Hills were exposed to the full fury of the hurricane-force winds. Trees which had survived extreme conditions over several centuries came crashing down without as much as a fight. The area around Shere and Ewhurst was badly affected, as this picture taken in Hound House Road shows. Surrey Advertiser photographer, Terry Habgood, inched his way along the lanes in his car, sometimes having to ease under fallen trees with much caution. North of Shere village is the Sheepleas beauty spot, which attracts scores of ramblers every weekend. Large portions of the wood were wiped out, and a year later, many trees were still lying on the ground as if someone had dropped a big box of matches from the sky.

Crunch! A tree smashes down on the roof of a house in Guildford. Shortly after the storm, MP David Howell visited the scenes of devastation around the town. He said afterwards he was impressed by the effort and energy which had been put into restoring electricity 'to tens of thousands of homes after the gale devastation'. He also praised the Army, Navy and Air Force who were called in to clear up in some of the worst-hit areas of the South East. In the Guildford area, an urgent plea was put out for more blood donors. Supplies had run low because of the storm and extra blood-doning sessions were arranged at Guildford, Cranleigh and Dorking.

Photograph: Surrey Advertiser

Lord Lieutenant of Surrey, Mr Richard Thornton, surveys the damage on his Hampton Estate at Seale, between Guildford and Farnham, and pauses to chat with the tree-sawers who were faced with a mammoth task in trying to clear the ruined woodland.

Photograph: Surrey Advertiser

Many Surrey town centres were a sea of debris as people fought their way to work on that memorable morning. Outside the shops — many of them still shut without any explanation in the window — pavements and forecourts were carpeted with parts of roofs, broken advertisement boards and tattered branches. This was the scene behind the Gateways super-market in Cranleigh.

Kingston, Surbiton and Hook

THE tree gang, employed by the London Borough of Kingston upon Thames, was alerted early on Friday morning October 16. A large beech had toppled spectacularly across the A243 at Chessington crashing over the Barwell café and the Leatherhead Road a short walk from the Zoo.

The gang, used to emergency calls, located the fallen giant. It was just past 1am. The wind was blowing furiously, increasing in its intensity and the men feared more trees might topple.

How right they were. During this crazy night more than 800 trees fell across Kingston's roads. One emergency call followed another and the pager carried by the parks department deputy supervisor, Terry Hamilton, bleeped almost continuously as his wife, at home, monitored the calls for help.

By 3.30 Tony Howard, supervisor of the tree gang realised he was in the centre of an emergency without precedent in Kingston's history. He called parks officer, Roy Boot. "We need help, the storm is worsening".

All parks staff and council workers from other departments were summoned to the Guildhall which was quickly turned into a control centre. Outside contractors were called in and scores of tree gangs were formed with the simple advice — "clear the roads but avoid loss of life"!

With the winds howling and the trees falling the gangs worked on. The emergency radio link-up system broke, but a policeman offered use of his walkie-talkie and a new system was devised whereby calls could be logged. Tree clearance work was hampered by a lack of vehicles and cutting equipment. Volunteers made hazardous journeys to Woking and even Sussex to collect more gear.

By dawn the storm had abated and the people of Kingston surveyed the damage, unaware at the time of the many men involved in the drama of the night.

Like the rest of Surrey, Kingston was plunged into darkness. There was serious damage to Tolworth Infants and Junior School and the Guildhall itself had to be roped off to prevent passers-by being hit by falling debris. Near Ham a large area of sheet aluminium covering the Assembly Hall at Tiffin Girls' School was ripped off. 475 council houses and 121 schools and colleges were damaged and Kingston's repair bill soared to more than £½ million.

At Chessington Zoo two huge marquees were ripped to shreds but Hook escaped with one blocked road, a few demolished walls and a bearded collie was so terrified that it whimpered all night long.

The men of Kingston didn't whimper. For three weeks after the storm they toiled to clear the roads.

The River Thames saw some dramatic scenes right the way up to its mouth at Southend. Near Kingston Bridge, Turk's boatyard was beaten savagely by the winds, and lost a number of windows and tiles, while the moored boats had their awnings, lifebelts and life-rafts torn off and swept away in the swollen river.

Sadly, the storm brought out the criminals, and there were reports of thefts of building materials from various locations in the borough. In Chessington, Father Brian Maxwell of St Catherine of Sienna Church, caught a thief red-handed as he tried to steal tiles from the Hempstow and Leggett yard in Leatherhead Road.

Photograph: Paul Adams

A typical surburban road near Surbiton. An uprooted tree in Cotterill Road, Tolworth, clubbed a family's car.

Lamp-posts were bent over like drinking straws as trees hammered down on Kingston Hill and Coombe Hill. Kingston Fire Station answered 30 calls for help during Friday October 16 and even the home of Kingston Council — The Guildhall — was a victim. Several tiles were blown loose and the building had to be roped off.

Kew will recover

NOWHERE in the storm-ravaged south-east evoked more public concern and sorrow than Kew Gardens when the extent of the damage was realised.

The Queen received a message of condolence from the secretary of the Royal Botanic Gardens, Michael King. In 1959 she had planted an English Walnut tree to commemorate Kew's 200th anniversary. Together with 1000 other trees it was felled by the freak weather conditions. Another victim was a Japonica planted by the Emperor Hirohito of Japan in October 1971.

Rare trees such as the Himalayan Elm which had survived Dutch Elm disease, and the finest specimen in Britain of the Californian Bay succumbed to the manic gusts of wind. Kew's most famous tree the living fossil, Maidenhair, was moved to Kew in 1761 two years after the garden was created by Princess Augusta, mother of George III. The tree remained upright but a branch was torn off.

Although Kew suffered a catastrophe the storm has enabled researchers to look at the root systems of exotic trees, and biochemists are studying the trees for potentially useful chemicals as well as the fungi which live in symbiotic association with the roots. The numerous fallen trees have meant that scientists can now examine the tree rings within the trunks and study the effects of climate and pollution on growth.

Kew will recover. Some trees may be re-established by propagation, and careful nurture of seedlings and saplings will ensure the gaps are filled. Kew will live on though the vista has changed.

Photograph: Surrey Comet

Still standing after the wild wind was the famous pagoda, towering 163 feet above Kew Gardens. Arthur Mee wrote in 1938: 'All the world comes to Kew. In lilac time or bluebell time or any other time, it is a matchless place.' Sadly, on the night of October 16 1987, the hurricane also came to Kew.

Photograph: Surrey Comet

Nearly 1,000 trees toppled over in Kew Gardens which hundreds of tourists to London and Surrey visit each day. For the staff and curator, it was the loss of a lifetime's work, as precious specimens were torn apart. So great were the shock waves caused by the news of the storm, that messages of sympathy arrived from foreign governments. Pictured above is the 1837 King William Temple at Kew which was battered in the tempest.

It was one of the saddest days in the life of Mr John Simmons, curator of Kew Gardens. But on surveying the devastation in the 300-acre grounds, he was amazed to find that the 200-year old trees established by Princess Augusta in the 1700s, when the gardens were set out, were undamaged, even though about 1000 other trees were uprooted.

Photograph: Surrey Comet

Staff of Richmond Borough Council worked all hours of the day and night to remove an estimated 2,000 trees which fell on roads and paths in the borough. This was the scene in a road at Teddington. A borough council lorry and bulldozer battle to clear the debris from around a crumpled car.

Photograph: Surrey Comet

A Ford Orion parked in this turn-of-the-century road in Teddington was demolished when a tree fell on the roof leaving the rear head-rests sticking out into the night sky, and a huge crater in the pavement.

Epsom, Ewell & Banstead

AT the height of the gale, dozens of ladies' shoes were hurled across Epsom High Street as the powerful winds smashed a plate glass window and sucked out many pairs of shoes. Some even reached the bank over the road. The manager of Mansfields, Mr Don Fentum, was called out from his Ewell home by the police at 4am but his route was blocked by fallen trees. On the downs, the winds tore over the grassy slopes, smashing greenhouses in Downs Wood and tearing off half the roof of Epsom Downs First School.

An ancient cedar crashed down at The Cedars in Church Street, and many people were trapped in their homes. In the big clear up that followed there was a queue at one stage of more than a mile long at the Longmead tip as people brought along their personal debris.

So many trees fell in Downs Road which links the town to the Grandstand, that it was impassable, and at Woodcote Side, a tree fell across a bungalow. In Ewell, a tree narrowly missed hitting ponies in a stable at Grafton Road. Fortunately, the animals were not hurt, but a horse trailer was demolished.

Banstead High Street was a scene of chaos, with a tree falling against Preedy's newsagent's in the Village, and another tree blocking the pavement near to the First School. In nearby Chipstead, the Long Plantation was flattened and a tree fell over a house in Hazelwood Lane. Shabden Park and Tickners Wood lost thousands of trees and a few months later, all that remained were muddy fields. Thousands of tiles were ripped off houses in Banstead Road, linking Woodmansterne with Carshalton, and one in three Banstead Council houses were damaged.

In Ewell many cars were crushed by trees, and Epsom Council estimated that the clearing up operation had cost at least £175,000.

In early November, the two famous trees in The Cedars at Epsom were removed using a 30 ton crane. One of the trunks weighed eight tons, and it was expected to be used for furniture.

Many historic trees crashed to the ground in Nonsuch Park, once home of a unique palace built by Henry VIII, now a park visited each weekend by hundreds of people.

Photograph: Epsom Herald.

Men and machine work swiftly to clear Ashley Road, Epsom. A typical Surrey scene during the days that followed the storm.

Photograph: Gordon Allis, Banstead Herald

Two victims in the same road after a night of terror in the Oaks Park area of Woodmansterne and Carshalton. At the height of the storm, Wallington's firemen were trapped here and had to flee to safety.

Photographs: Bob Jackson.

The day of the storm ... Christopher Horton, aged 16, was asleep at his home in Tadorne Road, Tadworth, when a huge tree smashed down on to the roof, causing extensive damage. Christopher's father was in a deep slumber and apparently did not hear a thing. Inset shows the house back to normal after ten months' building work.

Photograph: John Stuart, Banstead Herald

Banstead is mentioned in old guide books as being a large village on the North Downs, well-liked for its salubrious air. When that air travels at 100 miles an hour, it can be most unfriendly, as this bus shelter knows.

Sutton, Carshalton and Wallington

THE Borough of Sutton felt the full force of the storm as it swept down from the Surrey Hills. The parks and woodland areas that make Sutton one of the more sylvan of London Boroughs, were torn apart with a loss of over 50,000 trees. A further 7,000 fell on Sutton's streets. Oaks Park, Carshalton, alone lost 15,000 and six teams of tree surgeons were brought in from the Midlands to help out the council's own beleaguered workmen.

In just a few hours 1,000 council homes or 10 per cent of its total were damaged and with 2,000 trees across the roads 100 lamp columns were destroyed. Wallington fire station had a record 67 call-outs in under 48 hours. Some 2,500 children had at least one day off school.

Virtually every part of the Borough had a story to tell. At Roundshaw hundreds of residents were left completely exposed to the ravages of the storm as some 700 yards of a unique roofing material made of aluminium was blown high into the swirling skies and council officers were unable to retrieve it. Most of it was never found.

At St Philomena's School, when a tree blew down in 1973, a cache of human bones was found. It caused a nationwide stir. In October 1987 no more bones were discovered but the school grounds lost 79 mature trees.

One family must certainly feel that they had the most miraculous escape. Five year old Carla was asleep in her Carshalton High Street home, when she was awoken by the furious gusts of wind. She was on the top bunk bed and climbed down to her six year old sister and within seconds the ceiling fell in, showering the top bunk with debris.

They ran into their mother Deborah's room and seconds later a tree crashed into their bedroom. The mother grabbed the girls and ran to safety — not a moment too soon, for a chimney stack crashed into her room.

No cost can be put on to human life but the council faced damage to their property of more than £1 million with ongoing budgets for another £½ million, but it will take several years to clear the woodland sites, especially at Oaks Park.

As if the storm was not enough, residents had further worries the following Tuesday, when some 34mm (1.4″) of rain fell in the Wandle Valley and the river burst its banks, flooding Beddington Park and stopping trains.

Photograph: Surrey Herald

Trees litter the railway line between Walton and Weybridge. The scene was a familar one on all sections of the Southern Region and on the stretch of track between Reigate and Redhill 50 trees fell in the space of two miles.

Photographer John Stuart of The Sutton Herald climbed five floors of scaffolding to get this bird's eye view of Devonshire Road, Sutton, where a glade of pine trees had collapsed over the street, crushing two cars.

Photograph: Gordon Allis, Epsom Herald

The scene in the grounds of The Cedars, Church Street, Epsom. As in so many cases, it was fortunate that no one was around at the time. East Surrey Hospital at Redhill said after the storm that if the tempest had occurred four hours later, the local mortuary would have been filled to capacity.

Photograph Gordon Allis, Epsom Herald.

Mayhem at Epsom Downs where trees, walls and lamp-posts together collapsed in a tangled heap.

John Dauncey of Downs Wood, Epsom Downs in his greenhouse — what's left of it.

Photograph: Bob Jackson

Standing at the top of Epsom Downs, close to the racecourse, this building which stored office equipment had withstood many gales. On the morning of October 16 it collapsed like a marathon runner at the winning post.

Polesden Lacey, once the home of dramatist Richard Sheridan and where Queen Elizabeth, the Queen Mother and the late King George VI enjoyed their honeymoon, suffered badly in the storm. For a long time the gardens were less than majestic but nature, with a little assistance from the National Trust gardeners, is performing new miracles. The house is the headquarters of the Trust's southern region.

Camberley, Yateley and Windlesham

ONE drama followed another in the village of Windlesham, near Camberley where a gas leak was reported in a large secluded mansion and the emergency services could not get through because of fallen trees. At 10.40 am an explosion blasted the house, causing extensive damage to the upper floors.

Camberley firemen had been called to the house at 7.30 where they discovered a small fire in the boiler room. It was quickly dealt with but the crew sent a message to the North Thames Gas Board alerting them to a possible leak. The Board would normally have sent an engineer immediately but the roads were blocked and it was 11 am before he reached the house . . . too late.

The fire raged for hours and one fireman was injured when the roof collapsed.

For reporter, Barbara MacDonald of the Camberley News it was a memorable day. She was up at 4.30 am to investigate the chaos outside and when she arrived at the office to cover the storm of the century she heard the news of the fire. Busy Barbara had another message. A tree had fallen on her husband, breaking his leg.

Around the Camberley and Yateley district about one home in ten suffered damage and for many hours all roads out of both towns were blocked by fallen trees. Surrey Heath Council sent 45 men to cope with emergencies and they actually removed 190 fallen trees by 10.30 am.

At Blackbushe Airport, staff spent most of the night trying to prevent aircraft from being blown away but a Cessna trainer was damaged. At Sandhurst one driver got an unpleasant surprise when he came across power lines stretched across the road and saw they were alive just above his bonnet. He waved down other drivers but one ignored him and sped through leaving a trail of blue sparks.

Barograph Trace From Camberley During The Week Of The Big Storm. By K. Hustwick.

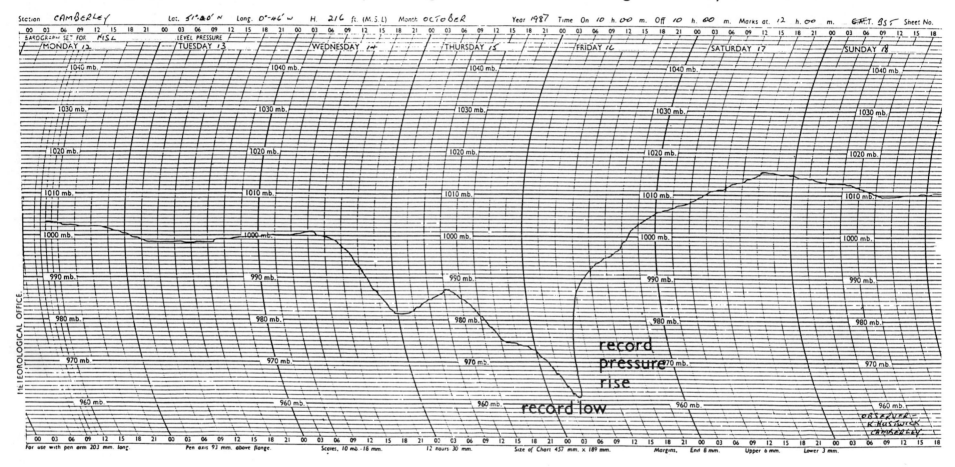

The huge dip in the graph shows how an incredible drop in pressure occurred in the early hours of Friday, October 16th 1987 over the Surrey area. This record lowest barometric reading for October was measured by Mr Kenneth Hustwick at his weather station in Camberley on the north-west edge of the county.

Photograph: Camberley News

Householders in Frimley spent the day sawing up a fir tree which had stormed into their garage and damaged the roof.

Photograph: Camberley News

A huge poplar tree crashed on to the home of pensioner Mrs Doris Butler in Manor Park Drive, Yateley, on the Surrey and Hampshire border, close to Camberley, bringing down electricity cables.

Photograph: Camberley News

The wrought iron gate was mangled when this multi-ton beech tree crashed just off Park Road, Camberley. The garage, only a few feet away, lost tiles and guttering.

Chertsey/Thorpe/Virginia Water/ Addlestone

IT was a miracle that so few people were killed in Surrey during the night of the wildest winds ever known. For scores of people, however, death was only a few inches away.

At Addlestone, a small baby was snatched to safety after a bedroom was demolished at the height of the storm. Little Samuel Lawes of Sayes Court, was saved by his strongly-built cot as the ceiling caved in under the weight of a tree. His mother, Sue, plucked him from the cot which was was almost buried in the smouldering debris. Unbelievably, Samuel was only slightly bruised.

The drama had an ironic twist to it for the baby's father, Howard, is a professional weatherman and well aware how savage an area of low pressure can be.

Three trees fell on the Lawes' house and the house next door. However they escaped lightly compared to one neighbour whose home was so badly damaged he had to be found alternative accommodation. Sensibly, to prevent further casualties in the road, signs were put up warning people to stay away.

Almost a year later, Runnymede Council was still counting the cost of the storm and the floods which resulted when the Medlake and the Bourne burst their banks. Staff had to work night and day for almost a month to control the effects of the severe weather.

Some of the huge costs incurred in clearing up were eased a little by the sale of usable timber, which was stored at Runnymede Pleasure Ground, but much of the wood was in poor condition so a big timber dump was set up at Chertsey Meads. Council staff worked until Christmas Eve tidying up grass verges which were littered with storm debris.

It was estimated in June 1988 that clearing Runnymede's roads had cost £61,000, and that repairing street lights, wounded trees and other victims of the gale had cost £160,000. In addition footpaths and bridleways, had been opened and new trees planted at a cost of £36,000. After repairs had been carried out to council properties, the final storm damage bill had risen to nearly £¼ million.

Egham, Staines, Ashford, Laleham

CRUSHED cars, crushed homes, impatient motorists, horrendous chaos and many more miracles. This was the situation near the Surrey/Middlesex border where one casualty was actually ignored — a sad-looking teddy bear in a flattened car.

There were more important matters for the rescue services — a woman trapped for two days at Barley Mow Road, Egham, the flood-water along Blays Lane, Englefield Green, flowing faster than the Thames and the occupants in homes throughout the district where roofs had peeled off like sardine tin lids.

A tree fell on the home of pensioner, Flora Harrison, tumbling masonry cracking the walls and at Riverside Road, Staines, Neil Richardson thought an aircraft from Heathrow had crashed on his house. Two boats at Thamesway, Staines were severely damaged and a youth at Shepperton was knocked unconscious when a beech tree fell on his motorbike.

Cherish the memory

A message from Sir Geoffrey Howe, Foreign Secretary and MP for East Surrey

WHEN the great hurricane struck Surrey I was in Vancouver attending the Commonwealth Heads of Government meeting. So the first news that I had of the disaster was when I turned on my breakfast television programme. I could not believe my eyes as I saw the pictures of Britons struggling through city squares and along country roads, as though through a tropical jungle.

A week later, when I returned to my constituency, the actuality was even worse than the report. Nowhere was worse hit than my official country residence at Chevening, just over the Surrey border in Kent — where thousands of trees, almost one third of the total were destroyed. And I found my House of Commons secretary and my Constituency Office, overwhelmed with cries for help from people living throughout East Surrey — help with their broken telephone lines, their disconnected electricity system, their long-obstructed local lane. The clamour of disconcerted citizens was understandably immense.

It fell to my office, and those who help me, to pass on these many requests for help to the various local and statutory Authorities. I have to say, that they and I were continuously delighted by the speed and courtesy with which the requests for help were dealt. If we have to denounce the elements for the savagery of the damage inflicted by the hurricane, then we have to thank our friends and neighbours, all those who worked on the roads, on the telephone lines, with the Electricity Boards, in the Army — and in a host of local services — for all the marvellous work which they did to bring life back to normal with such dramatic completeness.

This interesting book contains many photographs and other reminders of that night of windswept disaster. Let us cherish the memory and pay tribute to all those volunteers and workers who cleared the woodlands of Surrey of the devastated trees and branches; and convey our grateful thanks to all those Groups and Organisations who are committed to restoring Surrey to the beautifully wooded countryside that once we shared.

Photograph: Surrey Herald

Many hands make light work and for these two youngsters from Sheerwater Road, Woodham, they must have slept like a log after all their exertions. The Woodham area near Byfleet was badly hit with hundreds of trees being wiped out from the New Zealand golf course.

Photograph: Surrey Herald

Thanks to this chainsaw gang, a £265,000 international golf tournament was able to go ahead at the famous Wentworth course near Virgina Water. Days before the storm, the west side of the course was under five inches of floodwater, so when the hurricane struck, there seemed little hope of the event taking place. Half the tented village was blown away and more than 300 trees uprooted. Mr Kevin Munt, the course's new superintendent, and his 15 green-keeping staff became lumberjacks for the week and worked flat out to clear the ground. Champion Ian Woosnam, Britain's first winner in the event's 24-year history presented the team with a case of champagne.

Photograph: Surrey Herald Group

Thousands of pounds worth of damage occurred at Staines Rugby Club after several large trees fell on the timber building, wrecking the roof in four different places. In Pavilion Gardens, Staines, most residents had their cars trapped or damaged by fallen trees and as the dust settled after the storm, the Staines Town Society called on Spelthorne Council to back a tree-planting campaign. At nearby Laleham, a man who had just returned from war-torn Afghanistan, where he survived crossfire, could have been killed in his own bed back home if the 90 foot conifer outside his house had fallen the wrong way in the great gale. Tony Ashdown, of Church Cottage, was asleep when the tree crashed down against the memorial in the village. In Afghanistan, he missed being hit by a bullet, by just 12 inches.

Great Storm of 1703 in Surrey

OCTOBER 1987 was not the first time the fury of hurricane force winds was felt by the people of Surrey and the South East. In 1703 a dreadful tempest struck in the middle of a dark November night with such violence that 21 people were killed and 200 badly wounded in London alone.

The writer Daniel Defoe, of Robinson Crusoe fame, who was living in the city at the time, captured the horror of the storm in a documentary account published in 1704. It had the expressive title 'The Storm or a collection of the Most Remarkable Casualties and Disasters which happened in the late Dreadful Tempest both by Sea and Land'.

From his evidence we know that a deep and vigorous low pressure system swept north east across England on Thursday November 25. Defoe's own barometer was reading so low that he thought his children had broken it.

The storm intensified after midnight and by 2am on the 26th most people were awoken by the sound of falling masonry and tiles being hurled against their walls or through windows. But no-one dared to go outside, such was the fury of the storm which reached its peak around 5am. Defoe wrote that if it had continued for much longer nothing would have survived. When people finally ventured from the remains of their homes nobody could believe '... the hundreth part they saw'. Many houses were completely demolished and several thousand lost chimneys and roofs.

Surrey was battered by the storm. At Kingston-upon-Thames there was a miraculous escape when two children left their beds only seconds before a massive chimney stack fell through the roof. Kingston also suffered terrible damage to trees. One man lost 100 apple trees in his orchard. A new malthouse was demolished and All Saint's Church has been steeple-less since.

From Bagshot in Surrey came reports of huge elms torn up by the roots and many of the town's houses were damaged. The Manor House lost its chimneys and 400 panels of wooden stakes and some of its brick walls were demolished.

At Ewell near Epsom, lead from the house of a Mr Williams weighing an estimated 10 tons was blown over a ten-foot wall and landed 30 yards away.

John Evelyn, a writer who devoted much time to gardening and the study of trees, lived at Wotton between Abinger and Dorking. He wrote of the storm in his work 'The Pilgrims Way'. It blew down some two thousand of his finest trees and in his words 'subverted so many godly oaks prostrating them in ghostly postures, like whole regiments fallen in battle by the sword of the conqueror and crushing all that grew beneath them'.

Reigate was pulverised by the storm, with a vast number of tall trees blown down and one person wrote 'some were split asunder even though of considerable bigness'. At nearby Charlwood a miller who was worried about his windmill left his bed to turn the sails to the wind to avoid damage. He felt in his pocket for the key but had left it back in his house. On returning to the mill he found it completely demolished.

The Surrey countryside was devastated with barns blown down and corn and hay stacks moved great distances, many torn to shreds. At Capel not far from Dorking a family were in bed when part of their house collapsed, killing the husband and one child, but his wife and other child escaped miraculously.

One of the most dramatic stories from 1703 was the loss of the Eddystone Lighthouse. The builder Winstanley had realised in 1698 that it needed to be raised higher and strengthened and this was duly carried out.

In order to check the improvements he set out for the reef on the Thursday. When the seas abated after the storm there was no trace of him, his workmen or the keepers and the lighthouse was obliterated. Ironically at the same time Winstanley's house in Essex was destroyed as well.

The final, somewhat arbitrary death-toll was 123 on land, including the Bishop of Wells struck by a falling chimney stack, whilst he lay asleep. Conditions were even worse at sea and there was a colossal loss of life. As many as 8,000 overcome by mountainous seas and floods.

The grey light of that November dawn revealed a changed world with whole communities torn apart. And nearly three centuries later the same feelings of horror and amazement were felt by the people of Surrey after a night when hurricane force winds roared in from the ocean.

The highest point in South-East England is Leith Hill, 965 feet above sea level. Thousands of trees on the south-facing wooded slopes were left looking like a battlefield, and the nearby village of Coldharbour was cut off for days. Surrey Fire Brigade control room officer Miss Ann Lipsombe walked for four hours through a tangled jungle of trees in a bid to get to work in Reigate. At one stage she had to scramble up steep banks. Surrey firemen answered 1,250 distress calls in one day. County-wide, about 2 million trees fell.

Salt blew in from the sea

CROYDON is a borough of contrasts with its Manhattan-like tower blocks in the centre and farmland in the south. It boasts many open spaces and parks such as Addington Hills, Coulsdon Common, Farthing Downs and Lloyd Park. Nowhere was safe as the hurricane force winds roared in from the Channel.

The obvious casualties were the trees. A staggering 70,000 toppled in the parks and open spaces and a further 5,000 lining the roads and streets. So strong were the winds that windows and cars were covered by a layer of sea salt blown 40 miles inland. In parts of Coulsdon residents could hardly see out of south-facing windows. Some 100 roads were blocked. Buildings, too, were blitzed with more than 3,500 council homes damaged; about 20 per cent of the total.

The Borough of Croydon puts the storm cost at well over £1.5 million and nearly a year later council workmen were still attending to damaged bus shelters and park pavilions.

Like most of Surrey, Croydon was blacked out in the early hours, though luckily by noon many homes were back 'on stream'. Some houses, though, were still without supplies on the following Monday and a spokesman for Seeboard said it was the worst situation the borough had ever known.

The most tragic incident of all was the death of a motorist just after 6am on the Brighton Road. A massive tree came crashing down on a Ford Granada and the five occupants including an eleven year old boy were trapped in the wreckage. Men rushed out from a nearby post office and with help from a lorry driver the occupants were freed, but sadly the car driver died from his injuries. His passengers were treated at Mayday Hospital, Thornton Heath, and later released, the lad suffering only bruising and shock. The family were on their way to Gatwick to start their holiday.

Although many roads were blocked, the ambulance service kept going right through the storm. Two Addington ambulance men, John Buller and Del Jakeman, used every avenue to try and take a patient to Bromley Hospital. They even resorted to pushing the ambulance through a field with firemen hacking at fallen branches to clear a path. They probably saved the life of Addington resident Mr Mather, of Field Way.

There were some Croydonians who were happy about the weather conditions. They were the borough's children who had an extra holiday. Three-quarters of Croydon's 120 schools were closed.

A Fun Run was due to take place on the Sunday following the storm with more than 2,000 runners expected to take part in the event at Shirley Hills, but it had to be cancelled as there was so much damage along the proposed route. Indeed there were fears for the safety of the competitors.

Like neighbouring Sutton, Croydon also experienced further freak conditions on the following Tuesday. More than 1″ of rain fell during the day. Coulsdon was badly hit with four feet of water blocking the route on to the A23 at Marlpit Lane. Some cars were actually afloat in the flood-water. Flooding at Mitcham Junction meant trains were cancelled between West Croydon and Wimbledon. Croydon fire crews answered 207 flood calls as the River Wandle burst its banks inundating areas already clogged with fallen trees.

When the dust had settled, the winds abated and flood waters receded, the oldest living resident of Croydon was still standing proud. The sturdy cedar in the grounds of the Royal School of Church Music in Addington Palace at Gravel Hill is thought to be over 250 years old, but survived the storm and may well take on the next big tempest in the centuries to come!

Photograph: Ian Currie.

Luckily, this summer house was not occupied when it took off into the night sky, cleared a six foot high hedge and descended on a road in Woodcote near Purley, along with many trees.

Photograph: Croydon Advertiser Series

Virtually every tree-lined road had at least one casualty and this was a typical scene in Purley's leafy streets.

Two vehicles hidden in the foliage at Hayling Park Road, South Croydon.

Photograph: David Scorer

Until midnight on October 16, 1987, the wood behind Reeves Rest Lodge in High Road, Upper Gatton, near Reigate Hill was a favourite habitat of greater and lesser spotted woodpeckers, wrens, jays, flycatchers and tree creepers. Next morning the birds had gone — and so had the wood! Today it is a muddy field of thistles.

Battered bridleways

by Barbara Baboulene

SURREY is a county famous for its great chalk downs, its many acres of beautiful woodlands and its horses. Long before the willow was wielded on the county's village greens and long before men were chasing a small white ball up the fairways of Wentworth, the springy turf of the downs was cluttered with horses. Racing, hacking and hunting are synonymous with Surrey.

For the horse-rider today the destruction of the woodlands is a tragedy. Many miles of bridleways have been closed forcing horse and rider on to the road where, sadly, accidents are all too common.

The Oaks Park at Carshalton was perhaps one of the worst areas hit, removing an entire and solitary ride completely, and turning the nearby busy roads into a death trap for riders heading to Banstead Downs — so much further away.

In Old Coulsdon the woods which run through to the Kenley Aerodrome road are also out of use and likely to remain so for several years. In comparison the acres of riding around Walton Heath and Epsom Downs, though disfigured by fallen trees, have much enjoyment to offer riders who box and trailer there in droves.

The picture on this page shows the woods running from Chaldon to Old Coulsdon, an area closed by the local authority but opened after weeks of hard work by residents and horse owners.

Kings Wood in Warlingham offers restricted riding and is full of once majestic trees lying pitifully on their sides. Ironically it is only now that we can appreciate their former greatness. Fortunately there is a variety of riding available at Riddlesdown, Woldingham, Warlingham and Addington Gallops, and these are in constant use.

Mother Nature, with man's assistance, is working slowly to repair the damage, but it will be many years before Surrey's beautiful bridleways are all in use again.

Photograph: Neil McGinn, Surrey Mirror.

Barbara Baboulene meets another obstacle in the woods near Old Coulsdon.

Woking, Chobham and Byfleet

THE rasping whine of the chainsaw became a familiar sound around Woking in the hours that followed the storm. For several confused days it was the gardens that echoed to the buzz. Weeks later the sound moved to the woods as foresters and lumberjacks administered the last rites to once-proud trees.

The villagers of Mayford, Knaphill, St John's, Pyrford and Byfleet still recall how they were trapped in their homes on that fateful night, how Parvis Road and Cobham Road between Byfleet and the A3 roundabout were a scene of utmost chaos and how this awesome power had cut a great swathe through their countryside.

In Parvis Road, a man was blown off his bicycle and run over by a following car. He was found lying by the side of the road. An ambulance was alerted but could not get through. The crew from Cobham clambered on foot over trees and across back gardens with their equipment. With their trolley bed they scaled fences to reach the injured man. He was taken to hospital in Chertsey.

In St John's, Mrs Dawn Smith of Martin Way heard a loud smashing noise and opened her son's bedroom door to find him crawling from under a maze of twigs and branches. A poplar was sticking through the ceiling. Student Philip Gibby heard the chimney crash on to his roof at Bolton Lane bringing down a shower of tiles and another student at nearby Horsell escaped injury when a tree rudely entered her room.

Woking's hard-pressed firemen went to help the occupants of a house in Oak Lane Road where the roof had blown off and in Oyster Lane, Byfleet where a tree had hit the house. They found cars crushed, scaffolding buckled and boats damaged on the Basingstoke Canal.

Commuters returned home when they found that no trains were leaving West Byfleet and Woking. There were 62 trees lying across one five-mile section of the line. In Woking some shops stayed closed all day where others operated with a skeleton staff. Old-timers spoke of the war-time spirit with no electricity, no 'phones and a blitzed landscape all around them.

In Chobham, West End, Bisley and Windlesham there was widespread destruction to the woodland. Farmer Stanley Green had to devise a makeshift apparatus to milk his cows and young soldiers from the Guards depot at Pirbright lent a hand to old soldiers at the Princess Christian Homes where there was no electricity.

Photograph: Gatwick Airport Ltd.

This lorry was blown over at Gatwick Airport. Air traffic controller Paul Tingley said that huge containers were smashing into buildings and jagged pieces went flying through the air. Personnel were withdrawn from the runway. At one stage the control tower 'was rocking from side to side'.

Photograph Croydon Advertiser.

A falling horse chestnut claims another storm victim — this time in Auckland Road, South Norwood.

Photograph: Bill Beminster.

Debris from the nearby tennis court raced down the field and hit the back of the net. Repairs were necessary for Woking tennis and football clubs.

The Chris Lane tennis centre in Woking was the victim of the weather for the second time in a year. In March, an 80 mph gust tore the dome from the clubhouse, causing £½ million worth of damage. The hurricane added another £350,000 to the bill. Mr Lane is seen here standing next to the twisted steel frame.

Surrey in the dark

WIDE areas of Surrey were plunged into darkness as the strongest winds ever known brought down thousands of power cables. In homes all over the county, radios crackled to an eerie silence, light bulbs flickered and then expired in their millions.

It was some weeks before the most remote homes had their electricity restored but thanks to Seeboard's 'Hurricane Force '87' — a huge emergency squad — many saw the light after just a few days.

Seeboard's West Surrey division covers an area from Guildford in the west to Betchworth in the east and from Chertsey in the north to Cranleigh in the south. Almost 60,000 out of 145,000 consumers in this area of 715 square kilometres were without power.

In some areas of Surrey the screaming winds reached 100 mph as they tore down power cables, bowled over poles and threw debris — including garden sheds — high into the air. Overhead cables arced dangerously before crashing to earth. The worst hit areas were Cranleigh, Capel, Betchworth, Ewhurst, Leith Hill, Dorking and Abinger.

Mr Keith Sutton, Seeboard's West Surrey customer services officer, and Mr John Burchell, divisional senior engineer, recalled the events that took place on that memorable night. John was called out at 2.30 am and found that fallen trees were blocking his route to Guildford. He drove on the pavement, reached his offices and opened up as part of the emergency procedure. The East Grinstead switchboard which normally intercepts calls, could not cope on its own.

John spoke to the control engineer over the phone and to his horror discovered all the 30,000 and 11,000 volt systems in the area had gone. All he had were two engineers, a linesman and a foreman. They had already been called out but had been trapped by fallen trees at Ashurst Wood and at Cranleigh. John advised them to return home, have a hot meal and be prepared to start again at 7 am. One of the men found his route home blocked and he was urged to find shelter quickly.

Keith Sutton was called out at 3am to open up the Guildford switchboard. By 3.45 he was joined by three colleagues and by 6.30 two more had successfully braved the vicious tail-end of the hurricane. One man left his home at Borden, Hampshire, at 3.30 am. Six and a half hours later, his body racked with exhaustion, he took his place at the switchboard for a full day's work.

So great was the emergency that, in little more than two weeks, the Guildford office took 30,000 calls from often desperate consumers. Emergency teams were drafted in from all over the country — from South Wales, Scotland, Tyne and Wear and Lancashire — and accommodation was quickly found. Some men stayed in small guest houses and others in the plush Gatwick Post House.

In this mammoth task of getting Surrey switched back on there were many heroes and tales of bravery. There were also foolish situations, exemplified by a member of the public who climbed an electricity pole to put the fuses back. The riot act was read to him by a senior engineer.

At Alfold, linesman Nigel Howlett from Cranleigh, suffered serious injuries when a tree bough fell on him. Fortunately he was wearing a helmet but he was out of action for many weeks. In Betchworth repair teams were shot at by a madman with a handgun. The headlights on their landrover were damaged and the man was taken to court. At Chertsey, an old lady was locked in her house for three days because she had electric catches on her doors.

Among the brave and the foolish were the impatient. The switchboard was inundated with calls from young mothers who were in a desperate plight when they discovered their modern appliances would not work. In stark contrast was the old lady who didn't complain once although she was without electricity for two months. 'I knew you would get around to me one day,' she said gratefully.

Some weeks after the storm Surrey was aglow again after the county's biggest emergency operation since the second world war. It involved hundreds of men, many of them finding the strength to continue for hour after hour without sleep.

Photograph: Surrey Advertiser

PEOPLE in the worst affected areas of Surrey suffered prolonged power cuts and those with freezers faced the prospect of losing a lot of food.

Mr Ray Bennett of Grinstead Butchers, Bramley near Guildford, heard a plea on the County Sound Radio for people with large freezers in unaffected areas. Could anyone offer space for rapidly thawing produce for many beleaguered homes?

Mr Bennett being a butcher had a large freezer and surprisingly his part of Bramley avoided the power cuts. He immediately contacted the radio station and he was able to offer 'cold comfort' to more than 80 people from all over the area.

The picture shows Mr Bennett inside his freezer stacking up the contents brought to him in response to his offer.

Photograph: Surrey Advertiser

Overhead electricity cables in Brookhurst Hill, near Ewhurst Bowling Club were dragged to the ground by the hysterical winds. Telephone and electricity supplies to villages in the Ewhurst area were badly hit and a generator was brought from Tunbridge Wells to provide some relief before a gang of eight men arrived to restore supplies.

Photograph: Dorking Advertiser

Mole Valley MP Kenneth Baker toured the wrecked woodlands in his constituency and said he was shocked at the devastation, but full of praise for the way the emergency services had coped. He is pictured at the Friday Street beauty spot near Holmbury St Mary.

AN ANEMOGRAPH TRACE FOR GATWICK AIRPORT 16th OCTOBER 1987

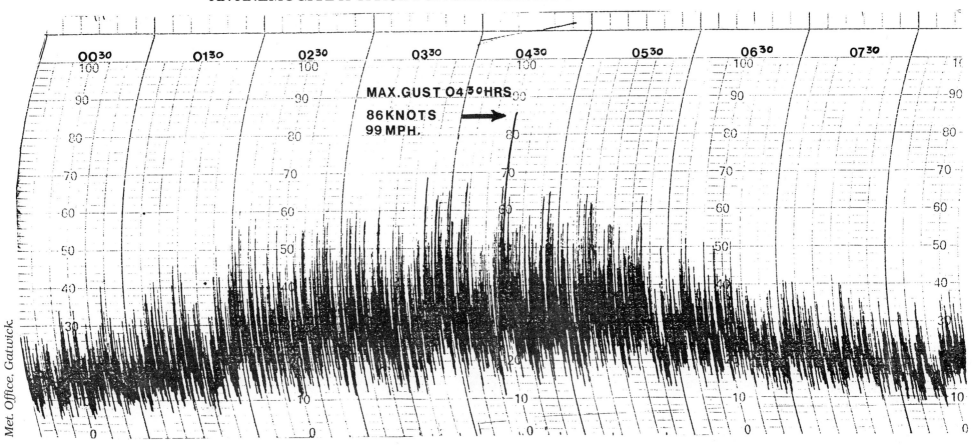

An anemograph is a record of wind speed, particularly useful in the detection of individual gusts which can cause so much havoc. In this example from the Gatwick Airport weather station near Horley, there is an 86 knot (99 mph) wind gust at 04.30 hrs GMT. The Meteorological Office believe this is a one-in-300-year occurrence.

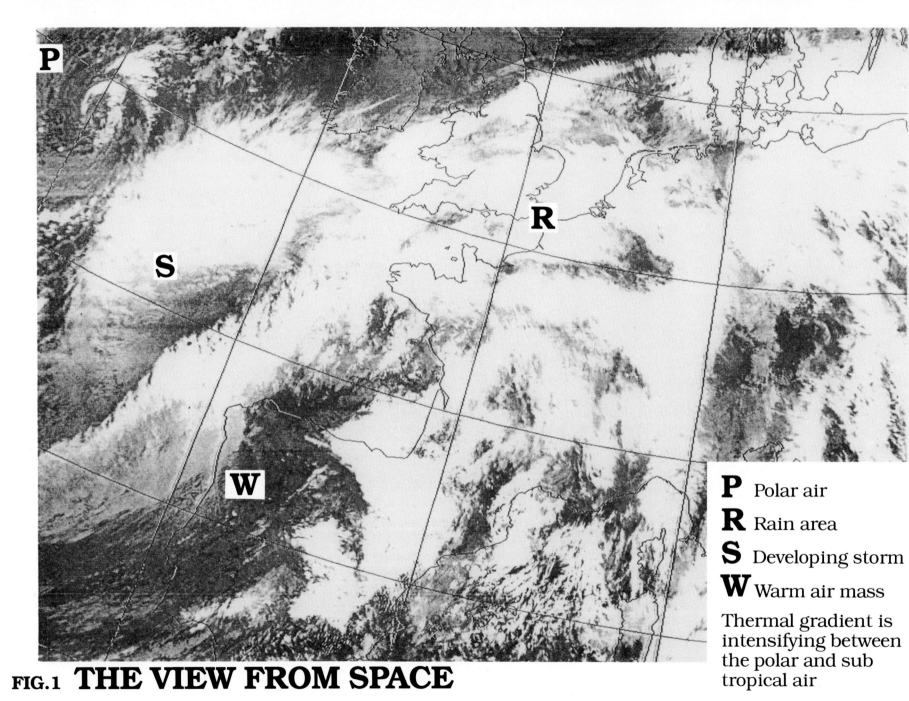

P Polar air
R Rain area
S Developing storm
W Warm air mass

Thermal gradient is intensifying between the polar and sub tropical air

Satellite: University of Dundee.

FIG.1 THE VIEW FROM SPACE

This was a satellite's view of the storm as it was forming over the Atlantic on the afternoon of Thursday October 15 1987.

Arkwright Road, Sanderstead. A new executive car was engulfed by one of the six sycamore and oak trees that fell across the road.

The Sanderstead roundabout looked like a battlefield. Drivers tried to circumnavigate this tree.

Photograph: David Scorer

A shop and flat at Purley Way, Waddon, Croydon. Business came to an abrupt halt

Life must go on and here commuters weave around an obstacle of fallen trees to get into Croydon just hours after the hurricane had passed. The scene is Waddon Road looking towards the heart of the old town.

Photograph: Treloen Penycate

High and dry at Hindhead. The wind is on its way towards the Surrey Hills.

Haslemere and Hindhead

PEOPLE in Hindhead mourned the death of a local resident from Beacon Hill who died in the storm. The motorist was found dead trapped in his car on the B2146 road between Petersfield and Chichester. He was discovered by tree-clearing gangs on the Friday morning. The front of his Ford Capri had been crushed by a large tree which toppled at Nursted Rocks. Emergency services took some time to get through because of the terrible state of the roads.

At Sun Vale in Haslemere, a tree crashed through the roof of a bungalow and through the window of a neighbouring house. Two old people in the bungalow woke up with a jump when a branch smashed through the ceiling. In the house next door, three children were unharmed as a branch broke their bedroom window filling the room with shattered glass.

Throughout the week that followed, many parts of the district were without lights, heat or water. Holy Cross and Haslemere hospitals managed to struggle on using generators, but for a long time Holy Cross was more concerned with the 17 trees which lay across the hospital drive.

Shopping was undertaken by candlelight and staff at Woolworths came up with the novel idea of mounting torches on headbands to help customers find the goods they wanted.

Near Haslemere's Mill Tavern, a pony died when a tree fell, crushing its stable.

STORM DRIVING

By Doug Nye

'COO, it is a bit breezy tonight', I thought as I walked to my car. It was just after 2am, the small hours of Friday morning, October 16 last. The night was black as pitch. Our porch-light swung crazily in the gathering gale. The swaying row of 30-foot high Cupressus beside our lane swished and roared, their din threatening in its intensity.

I settled myself into our brand-new (200-miles only) Renault 21 Savanna, and flipped the key.

In retrospect, that was my first mistake. Right then, I should have done the sensible thing — switched off, scuttled in to bed. But as a journalist, who often works by night, I had just finalised an urgent piece for *The Observer*, required without fail Friday a.m. The night-time whizz from Farnham to London is quite relaxing, a rare chance to think, free of phone and family — it can be fun ...

On to the main road, down towards Farnham itself. No other traffic, lonely, just the way I like it. But what's this? Twigs and leaves showered past in a sustained gust, the Savanna's wipers smearing sap across the screen.

Out on the bypass she suddenly veered in the cross-wind — a hollow traffic bollard, disembowelled, trailing wires, bounded across my path, chased by scattering shards of its own broken yellow perspex. Hmm, perhaps this wasn't just your ordinary gale ...

Up past Aldershot and Farnborough, by this time I'd adjusted my seat further forward to increase my upward field of vision through the screen. I was gazing up at the flailing roadside trees as much as forward at the road. Interesting choice. What speed is best? Slow enough to stop if you spot a toppling tree? Or quick enough to be in danger the least possible time? I opted well clear of the lee-side trees, kept in third or fourth to have instant acceleration on tap, concentrated on dodgeability.

Past Farnborough airfield a massive gust blasted me right-of-centreline. A storm of leaves, twigs, larger branches grapeshot by. A bough bounced off the screen with a deafening 'thwack' — I jumped as if shot. Now my heart was really thumping. Stuff *The Observer*?

No. Seemed daft to have come so far just to give up now.

So I pressed on.

The motorway felt safer — more open, despite assorted debris bowling across its carriageways. More traffic here waltzing in that irresistible wind.

Think forward — I'm not running clear of it, perhaps it's moving north-east with me. The Sunbury fly-over, high and exposed! Mmm. Don't fancy that. Should I opt for the minor roads below? Another mighty gust boomed around the otherwise astonishingly quiet Savanna. I'd inadvertently swapped lanes. There's greater threat from flying debris than of being blown over or off the road. More dicey then to be beneath the flyover than up on top of it?

I pressed on, over the top with the gale palpably right behind! My oh my, it was really blowing now.

On past Twickenham RFC, into Richmond. Now sizeable boughs lay downed, quivering on the road. Hammersmith flyover —piece of cake, blown along it, into the city. Red lights. I stopped in the right-hand lane, as far from the flanking trees as possible. A cabbie stopped alongside, we swopped grimaces. Branches down in Knightsbridge, a Harrods awning was all but torn away.

Dammit, muddled my route, found myself in Trafalgar Square. Apparently amiable young drunks hitching energetically, all leaning 45-degrees into a mighty gust. It abated. They fell down.

At last, around 3am, St Andrew's Hill ...there's the letter-box I want. I ducked from the car to deliver my envelope. A dustbin rumbled by, scattering papers, hoovered instantly way into the air. The gale boomed in those deep-valleyed city lanes. A crash and shatter of breaking glass nearby.

Back along the Embankment. Hefty sections of shattered tree part-blocked the road. Parliament Square, dammit, I'd lost myself again. Victoria Coach Station, flattened trees blocked the road, kerbump over the kerb —along the pavement —evenin' orl — I'm going home no matter what.

Into the teeth of the storm; back past Twickenham RFC — a truly *staggering* sight.

The dual-carriageway there had become just a nervous, twitching, shaggy green carpet of twigs and leaves. Larger boughs, fallen trees, humped into view merely as islands in the green, leafy tentacles flailing in the gale. I was weaving rapidly now, lock to lock, dodging the major obstacles. But they were all moving! Ripped-off boughs the size of decent Christmas trees went hurling bodily, left to right, clear across the road in front, four to five feet above ground.

I'm just going home.

A car ahead took a bough on its left-front — its brake lights flared red and angry, OK but stopping, reeling out of line like a torpedoed ship in a wartime convoy while its consorts steer round it, ploughing on. I'm just going home.

Sunbury flyover again, this time head into wind. Down into the dip, then up on to that familiar elevated left-hand curve. Suddenly there's a terrific gust. The steering's failed! The wheel went slack; my arms almost crossed!

Instantaneously I could only think I had hit some debris, broken the steering. Then brief squeal of rubber, the Savanna swerved. I corrected. It drove on normally. Presumably its front wheels had been lifted from the road ...

Capt'in — I don't like this game. Let's play another?

Beating back south-west along the M3 it was a struggle to push the Savanna above 55 into wind. At Longcross past the Chobham test-track hefty boughs were sprayed across both inside and centre lanes.

No way had the storm moved on. This was worse than ever. Farnborough, Aldershot, there's a nerve-racking narrow section beneath tall trees. I expected it to be bad. It was. A diffuse misty shape in the headlights. A fallen tree blocking the road completely. Ah there's a lay-by just here, just a car's width space to squeeze round the tree's top-most branches.

One hundred yards further on, another toppled giant. Up the kerb this time, past it on the grass verge. Still debris is showering down, across and all around. Fifty yards round the corner, another total block, but this time slap opposite a filling-station forecourt — in through the entrance, behind the pumps, out the exit and on we go.

I'm going home.

And at 4.10am I made it, only to find my own lane blocked by three fallen giant Cupressus — *my* fallen giant Cupressus. Reversing round the corner, I parked well away from the nearest tree and returned on foot to wrestle the wet and fallen trees aside. Then I retrieved the car, and parked it safely 'neath the lee of home.

Mere survival had been a lottery. I think one *can* drive in a manner which helps your chances, but if your number's up in such a storm, it's up. It helped just to think 'Lord, *please* get me home intact, and *please* let home and family be intact if I get there ...'.

Of one thing I am sure. Next time, I will post my copy.

Photograph: Farnham Herald

The axeman cometh! These branches stuck out into the road like aliens blown in by the storm, but this resident in Fuller's Road, Rowledge, near Farnham, was determined to keep them at bay.

Farnham

FOR many days after the storm candlelit dinners became a way of life for the beleaguered people of Farnham and its environs. There was no power for more than a week and those with log fires hosted many extraordinary evenings and never tired of exchanging stories of The Night.

Public houses also welcomed new customers, especially in those villages isolated by fallen trees. At one time all roads out of Farnham were blocked and the landscape was badly scarred. More than half of the 45 sewage pumping stations in the Waverley district were out of action and emergency generators were brought in from Oxford.

The district has the biggest acreage in Surrey and most of it is rural. Pine woods were torn to shreds, the slopes of Farnham Park lost 75 per cent of their mature trees, and a much-loved avenue of pink and white chestnuts were weeded out.

There were more tree casualties than almost any other part of Surrey and the Forestry Commission estimated that in the Alice Holt area, 7,000 tonnes of timber fell. The hills on the south side of the Hogs Back lost their oaks and beeches and Hampton Estate, home of the Lord Lieutenant, Richard Thornton was like a jungle and in Farnham itself cherished town trees were uprooted.

In the chaos which followed there were also chainsaw casualties and warnings from Southern Electricity of dangerously hanging live cables. At Tongham Moor two golden retrievers were electrocuted while walking with their mistress.

Buildings did not escape. A portable classroom was flattened at Weydon School and the gable ends of two bungalows were blown out at Tongham. One occupant had to be told by a neighbour that there was no wall on the other side of her wallpaper.

Community spirit glowed as brightly as the log fires. The villagers of Elstead led by Poppy Whitty and the Venture Scouts set up a soup kitchen, the Rev Clive Powley spent four hours directing traffic round a dangerous cable at Tongham, Gurkha soldiers from the Queen Elizabeth Barracks helped to clear trees at Crondall and Tony Russell, a sidesman from Farnham Church, spent long hours clearing Compton Woods with his bare hands.

Photograph: Farnham Herald

A great war-time spirit prevailed in the days after the great storm, but inevitably, there were a few stories which cast a shadow over the many tales of goodwill. In the village of Rowledge near Farnham, part of which is '50 yards into Hampshire', thieves stole the copper top of an ornate lamp from a lane leading to the church. It had been damaged in the gale, and the pieces were scattered on the ground. Above is Rev. David Eaton in his churchyard, holding the lamp parts.

Photograph: Farnham Herald

These towering evergreens were prised out of this garden in Boundstone Road, Farnham, and came thudding down on the roof. The lawn resembled an earthworks.

77

Photograph: Farnham Herald

Villagers at Rowledge, near Farnham, formed a big clear-up squad to rid the streets of its carpet of branches.

In the 1930's author Arthur Mee travelled the country visiting villages and making detailed notes for his books. He wrote of Puttenham in 1938: 'Almost on the slopes of the Hog's Back, it is a place of peace and charm, with a trim churchyard and a church so inviting that its altar cross can be seen from the road.' Very little of the church could be seen when numerous trees fell in the storm, blocking roads and isolating the village from the outside world. And there was certainly no peace and tranquility!

Photograph: Keith Harding

Stars Wood, Effingham was wiped out while evergreens in the garden of the house on the left escaped unscathed. A mile to the right is the National Trust's Surrey headquarters. Polesden Lacey.

Dorking and Leatherhead

A year after the storm large areas of woodland around Dorking and Leatherhead still bore the scars of that grisly night. Huge gaps of light were to be seen along the hillside landscape and, in the gardens below, hundreds of years' work erased by nature's fury. In the heart of the Surrey countryside they still talk about the storm and they will talk about it for generations to come.

In the Mole Valley the winds were wild and ruthless. Beauty spots like Sheep Leas, Friday Street, Ranmore and Effingham will take years to recover. The much-visited tourist spot of Leith Hill, where rhododendrons and azaleas were so profuse, now resembles heathland. Abinger Common has a similar appearance.

Stories will always be told about the many weeks without power in the rural villages and how British Telecom engineers from Scotland were still battling to repair mile upon mile of overhead cables in November. Roads, too, were blocked not for a day but several weeks.

Thousands of people in the Mole Valley lived without power for many days and that area was on red alert as the river level rose dangerously, spilling over the roads in Brockham. One hardware shop in Dorking sold 300 boxes of candles in five days.

At Headley Heath, Leatherhead pensioner Mrs Nora Bale and her husband were so frightened in their mobile home they decided to move to the summer house in the garden. There were no lights so they returned for a torch. It was a good decision to go together — a huge tree smashed the summer house into matchwood. The couple sat in their mobile home, praying all night.

Ida Haulkham of South Holmwood is another lady who will never forget the bizarre events of October 16. Suffering from an allergy she was in great pain and called for an ambulance which set off to Crawley Hospital just as the winds blew in.

At almost every turning an uprooted tree blocked the path of the crew so using a saw they cut their way through while Ida lay sedated in the ambulance.

Near Betchworth they climbed up Pebble Hill but the branch of a falling tree pierced the roof of the ambulance. Crew and patient abandoned the vehicle and looked for a house. Ida was carried over huge trunks and debris while the men struggled against the mad wind, almost side-stepping falling trees. She was put to bed. They survived, but wondered how.

A week later, Dorking rock band Ob Jay Da composed a haunting song called 'The Storm'.

So many trees fell across the A24 at Mickleham between Dorking and Leatherhead that drivers made a makeshift main road through the woods in a desperate bid to get to work. Three days' production of milk had to be poured down the drain at Norbury Park Farm, Mickleham, because of the loss of power. Landscape gardener, Mr Martin Burgess from the village heard of the farm's plight and lent his small hedge-trimmer generator to cool the milk.

Photograph: Dorking Advertiser

Thousands of acres of farmland and meadows were turned into raging torrents of water as the River Mole burst its banks at Leatherhead. A red flood alert was issued on Wednesday October 22 — less than a week after the hurricane, as freak torrential rain lashed down over Surrey, making it the wettest October of the century. Sandbags were issued to homes in danger, and although few properties were flooded, many roads were awash with mud, water and branches. This is the scene at Young Street, Leatherhead, on the day of the hurricane.

Insect and plant life may be altered for good in parts of Surrey. The green hound's tongue plant thrives in areas where light is obscured by beech trees, such as at Mickleham. The plant is very rare but has thrived in Mickleham for more than 300 years. This picture shows part of Givon's Grove which was once a densely populated wood. The trackways were turned into rivers of mud after the torrential rain which both preceded and followed the hurricane.

A teenager in Dorking was so shocked at the scene of devastation that he hurried round to his friend's house, woke him up and said: 'Quick, get up. The whole of Dorking's changed.' Here, in Ashcombe Road, which takes A25 traffic to Guildford, more than 30 trees fell. In Newdigate, pop star Hurricane Smith felt his house shake and admitted: 'I don't like wind!'

Photograph: Dorking Advertiser

Photograph: Malcolm Case Green, Dorking Advertiser

Dorking was cut off from Guildford by dozens of trees blocking the A25. Here, at the Westcott Road approach, an avenue of trees fell like dominoes. Several new saplings have been planted so that future generations can enjoy a scenic and leafy approach to the old market town.

Esher, Walton, Weybridge & Long Ditton

AT 3.30 am, the first of 10 gangs of council workmen set off from the Esher depot in the biggest emergency seen in the Borough of Elmbridge since the disastrous flooding of September 1968.

More then 1,000 trees had fallen along the highways. The pine woods at Oxshott were demolished and Seven Hills Road at Cobham an avenue of fallen trees. It was an unbelievable sight. One council workman nearly didn't reach the depot for he was twice blown off his bicycle while cycling in from Walton.

The Portsmouth Road between Cobham and Esher was impassable and Claygate was cut off from Hook by fallen trees in Red Lane and Woodstock Lane.

Calls to the police and firemen started about 2am and it was not long before the council's depot manager Mr Tom Green was called to deal with the effects of the worst storm for 284 years. At the height of the hurricane, Mr Green and other council officers were driving around to see for themselves the extent of the damage.

In Long Ditton, a telegraph pole had been punched to the ground by a falling tree, disconnecting phones for three weeks in homes up and down Ditton Hill Road. The tree struck a pre-war semi-detached house and the road had to be closed while a 25-ton crane removed the tree. Road closed signs could not be erected because the supply had run out. Trees also blocked the elegant St Mary's Road which leads to Surbiton, and those who reached the station there, were unable to get to London.

At Painshill Park, Cobham, buildings escaped but many of the 18th century trees were destroyed and the craters left behind when they toppled over wrecked the newly-restored lawns, paths and shrub beds. It was a blow for those who had worked long hours restoring the famous landscape gardens. Fortunately, the giant cedar trees survived, including the tree reputed to be the largest in the country.

Elmbridge Council later appealed to the public to keep out of the woods and off the commons, because of the dangerous state of the trees. In West End, a picture-postcard village tucked away behind Esher's many acres of firs, Mrs Nellie Johns, aged 80, woke to find a wall of her house had blown away. Thanks to neighbours, she was removed to safety.

At Cobham, early estimates were that 600 trees had fallen on or near roads, and on the old A3 road between Cobham and Esher, 21 had come down. The police station had to call in extra men to cope with all the calls, and then there was the added worry of flooding. The River Mole went on red alert for the third time in a fortnight and minor flooding occurred at Mill Road, Cobham, and at Plough Lane, Downside, where the river had burst its banks.

In Weybridge, the great storm brought an oak tree down on the home of Mr Kenneth Rogerson in Marlborough Drive. He and his wife, Joan rushed from their room but a second oak fell towards them, smashing another part of their home. Mr Rogerson saw it fall, and, with the house visibly shaking, they turned to run out of the back of the house but a pine tree fell towards them. Mr Rogerson, 73, said that as a navigator in the war, he had awards for being shot at and shot down. But at no time had he been more frightened than during the events of October 16 1987. The couple had to stay in temporary accommodation at the Seven Hills Motel in Cobham.

Photograph: British Telecom

A tree and a telegraph pole take a tumble together in Long Ditton.

Photograph: Surrey Herald.

A tale of Wou! This Mercedes was a victim of the violent winds in Weybridge.

Photograph: Surrey Herald

This detached house in Weybridge, and many others nearby, needed extensive roof repairs after trees were tugged out of the ground.

Oaks Park, Carshalton

FOR many people in South London and East Surrey the impact of the sheer power of the hurricane force winds was dramatically revealed at Oaks Park, Carshalton. Even now, nearly a year after the storm, passing motorists slow down and gaze in disbelief at the remains of the woodland. It was one of the worst hit areas in all southern England.

Oaks Park lost some 80 per cent of its trees. At least 15,000 were destroyed. Such was the loss it was even featured in the New York Times on October 22, where readers were told that the bill for this area alone would be 6.8 million dollars.

Oaks Park took its name from a group of massive old oak trees called the Lambert Oaks after the Lamberts of Banstead. Little is known prior to the eighteenth century when a house on this site was known to be used by a society of Gentlemen in the hunting season. It was owned by Sir John Burgoyne who fought in the American War of Independence.

In 1774 a spectacular and extravagant engagement party for the son of the Earl of Derby was held at the house known as The Oaks and when he succeeded as the 12th Earl, he bought the mansion, acquired its freehold, enclosed some common land and the Park was born. The famous Oaks and Derby horse races of nearby Epsom are connected with the house.

In the twentieth century the house lost its eminence and was badly bombed in the second world war. In the 1950's it was demolished but the gardens and parkland were opened to the public.

One person particularly upset by the wholesale destruction of the park is Robert Gilbert. He lived at The Oaks where his father Gabriel was head ground keeper. His father planted hundreds of trees, including an avenue of tall trees stretching away from the house. Although the house was pulled down he continued to win prizes and public acclaim for his flower displays in the newly designated public park.

After the storm, Robert Gilbert, now a resident of Nutfield, was almost in tears as he surveyed the nearly unrecognisable park. As a massive tree planting programme unfolds, Mr Gilbert wants to donate a new section in memory of his father.

The Oaks lost many of its beech trees and they typified the problems faced by trees growing on the thin chalky soils of the North Downs. The trees develop a shallow root system, especially those away from the edges of woodland where trees tend to develop a more extensive network of roots as they are subject to stronger winds.

With trees quite close together a domino effect takes place, with one tree bringing down another and so on. The wind can blow more strongly through the space created by the fallen trees. The soil on the night of the storm was soft and yielding due to an exceptional rainfall in the days beforehand. The trees themselves were still in full leaf and could not resist the mighty force of nature as it swept across the Park.

The damage was particularly concentrated along a shallow north-south valley, where a funnelling of the wind took place as it descended the dip slope of the Downs. There were also down gusts in the turbulent flow of air that could have initiated the felling of the first few trees.

I visited Oaks Park a few days after the storm. People were wandering about in stunned disbelief. One person I passed said 'How can you describe this to anyone? You can only look and wonder at the work of nature'. These same sentiments were expressed by Defoe after living through the Great Tempest of November 1703.

As I walked among the twisted, tangled mass of trunks and branches a squirrel was busily collecting his winter store of food.

Nature goes on regardless.

Photograph: Ian Currie

In memory of the 15,000 trees lost in four hours at Oaks Park near Woodmansterne.

Redhill, Reigate and Horley

JUST after midnight a cola can started to roll down Doods Road. It was followed, not long afterwards by milk bottles, then dustbin lids, cartwheeling crazily through the night. Two hours later the first of a succession of express trains thundered through the town centres of Redhill and Reigate.

At least, that's what it sounded like — a faraway whistle building up to a deafening, crashing roar and then peeling off across the North Downs, fading eerily into the distance. In those dynamic gusts no-one could hear the trees crashing and buildings collapsing. That was a sight for the morning.

Nine of the ten main roads around Reigate and Redhill were blocked. In Chart Way a fir tree crashed through the roof of Peter Clifford's bedroom. He was downstairs at the time. Natalie Barr, returning in her car from Horley, actually saw a tree falling. She dived on to the back seat as it smashed through the windscreen. Natalie was unscathed.

In Redhill a store in Hooley Lane was demolished, shop windows shattered and dozens of walls felled. On Redstone Hill, Redhill was cut off from Nutfield and a roof blown off in Fairhaven Road.

In Horley three flats and several cars were wrecked at Cranbourne Close, a tree pushed through the roof of a house in Horley Row, another at Honeycrock Court, Salfords and yet another at Copsleigh Avenue.

In the Tandridge area of Oxted, Limpsfield and Caterham there was terrible damage. An old people's home was virtually demolished at Blindley Heath when a chimney crashed through the stairwell. Firemen were called to evacuate the pensioners and another chimney stack crashed into the dining room. They had just moved with the nurses to another room.

Team manager, Mrs Mavis Bayley was amazed that none of the 22 residents were injured. They were given emergency accommodation in the nearby church hall.

In Oxted a huge tree crashed through the roof of the Red Cross Hall and a mighty crane had to lift it free. At St Michael's School, Limpsfield 27 trees keeled over, damaging windows and fences, a greenhouse and changing rooms. At Hazelwood School the chapel was demolished and classrooms smashed.

On Limpsfield Chart the army removed trees blocking Kent Hatch Road and the National Trust management team was brought in to assess the damage. They estimated the clearing up would take three years.

Photograph: Jeremy Quinton

A heavy plant endeavours to open the A25 at Redhill which was blocked by several trees, isolating the town from the village of Nutfield. Today the trees have been cleared from the ridge on the road to Bletchingley, creating many new viewpoints.

A Tale of Tragedy

A tale of tragedy emerged from Purley Way, Croydon, the morning after the storm, when a severely disabled resident was found dead by a home help. The 60-year-old woman's dog was pining by her body. It is thought she may have tried to get out of bed to check if the terrible winds had damaged her home, and in doing so, collapsed from her exertions. At first, it looked like her pet would have to be put down, but thanks to a lady in Colley Way, Reigate, the animal was given a new home.

Photograph: Surrey Mirror

In many parts of Surrey it was the wettest October of the century — adding to the misery. This was the A23 at Salfords, between Horley and Redhill, on Wednesday October 21 1987 after a tributary of the swollen River Mole turned the main road into a sea of mud, leaves and twigs. The bad weather continued into the winter, with January also being one of the wettest in the county this century.

Photograph: Alex Watson

This photograph was actually taken in Kent almost a year after the storm. It shows an expansive view from the greensand ridge at Ide Hill towards the East Surrey Water Company's reservoir at Bough Beech, a few miles from the border. The woodlands on the hills above the Weald were directly in the path of the storm. They were devastated.

Photograph: Surrey Mirror

Weather experts said that strictly speaking the storm was not a hurricane. Try telling this to the residents of Kingsley Grove, Hartswood, Reigate!

93

Photograph: Surrey Mirror

Two cars and a garage were destroyed with a single blow. This is Cronks Hill, Reigate on the Friday morning.

Ghost Train at Redhill

AS the London to Gatwick train pulled out of Victoria Station at 1.0 am dozens of holidaymakers slumped into their seats relieved that they had crossed London at last, and would soon be jetting off to sunnier climes. Little did they know that they were starting a journey that would turn out to be more frightening than any ghost train ride.

In little under 20 minutes they had passed East Croydon Station and within half an hour would be going up the escalators to the departure lounge. The outline of dark trees swaying in the wind made little impression, for soon this would be replaced by scenes of sparkling seas and blue skies.

Among the holidaymakers was journalist, Barry Patton, who had just finished a tiring day at the News International plant at Wapping. He wished he was going on holiday, but for the time being just wanted to get home and collapse into bed.

Suddenly, a terrific grinding noise filled the air and caused everyone to sit up. It got worse and as the train entered Merstham tunnel, the lights went out abruptly, and the train jerked to a halt. In the pitch darkness a message eventually got through that the train had hit a tree which had ploughed into the tunnel and was wrapped under the carriages.

Unable to see, the confused passengers waited and waited, but nothing happened. Cigarette lighters were lit, and in the dim glow, strangers talked to each other nervously. After 45 minutes fear set in. With the screams of wind whistling at the tunnel mouth, it became obvious that something serious was happening.

A diesel train arrived from Redhill and went up towards Croydon before coming down the track to push them through the tunnel to safety. But as they came out the other side, the nightmare really started. The train hit another tree which had fallen right across the cutting, on to the tracks. With winds howling as in a horror film, the passengers sat tight until two off-duty police officers and a railway guard told everyone they would have to abandon the train for their own safety.

They were ordered to leave their baggage behind and walk up the track, through the storm, to Merstham Station for protection. In the teeth of the storm, the passengers marched in a long line along the ballast between the rails for almost half a mile, helping the less capable. All around them trees were falling and there was the sound of breaking glass. Someone used an axe to hack down a gate near the station but there was little protection because of windows smashing, so they huddled under the pedestrian bridge. Many prayed.

When another train eventually arrived to rescue them, it, too, got cut off by trees near Earlswood and had to reverse to Redhill. There, the bedraggled passengers were led into the Post Office canteen but there were so many people, some had to sit on the steps. At this point, the lights went out and they had to leave for security reasons and get back on the stricken train where they spread towels and newspapers on the floor and tried to sleep. All around them windows and signs were smashing, and by now it was almost dawn. At 10 am they were put on to coaches and taken to Gatwick by way of numerous diversions. They were reunited with their luggage and eventually able to fly away from their ordeal.

For Barry Patton the journalist, who decided to run the four miles home from Merstham to Redhill it was a night he is lucky to have survived. While sprinting down the A23 in the howling gale, he turned to see an oak tree chasing him along the road. Leaping up a four foot garden wall, the tree overtook him and continued skimming along the London Road towards Gatton Point. Out of breath, Barry reached Redhill town centre which was alive with the sound of alarm bells ringing. Nearby, police were chasing airborne loft insulation and told him "he should not be out on a night like this." He agreed and told them he was going home!

FOR TV presenter Cliff Michelmore it was a day he will always look back on in amazement. Returning from the Isle of Wight to his Reigate home, he found Reigate Hill blocked by dozens of toppled trees, crumpled lamp-posts and mangled crash barriers. He and his radio presenter wife Jean Metcalfe were dumbfounded.

A year later, Mr Michelmore said. "I just hope the trees lost in Surrey will be replaced with oaks — and not simply flowering cherries."

THE South Eastern Electricity Board dealt with 25,000 faults in the aftermath of the hurricane. Three thousand poles fell and 700 miles of overhead line lay on the ground. Five thousand miles of cable were out of action and 50,000 fuses had to be replaced. At Guildford 800 rounds of sandwiches a day were made for repair gangs. Altogether, throughout the region, 8000 men were sent out to restore Surrey's power.

Photograph: Mrs J. Tyrell

There was mayhem in South Nutfield's Mid Street, while in 'Top' Nutfield, the A25 was littered with trees. Now, there are some open views across to the South Downs, but this was little consolation to the owners of these cars.

The morning after at The Red Cross Hall, Oxted. A massive crane had to lift this tree free.

Some of the damage caused to Dippen Hall in Blindley Heath near Lingfield when two chimney stacks crashed through the roof. Miraculously no-one was hurt, but the home, already earmarked for closure, had to shut down early.

Photograph: Horley Mirror

Five plate-glass windows were smashed as this horse-chestnut tree was wrenched out of the ground outside these flats near the Chequers roundabout on the A23 at Horley.

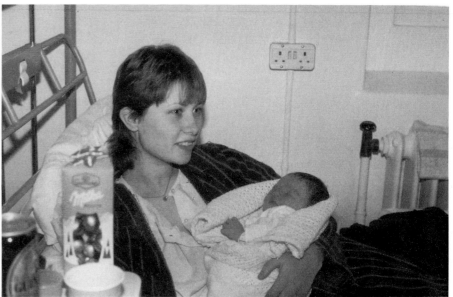

Storm Baby

JILLIAN Collingwood of Farncombe, near Godalming went to bed fearfully wondering if her baby would be born on such a wild and windy night.

As the storm gathered strength, she could hear trees tearing from the ground and then, all of a sudden, she started having contractions. Her fear had come true. Henry led her to the car and they set off headlong into the night. Every road leading out of the village was blocked by fallen trees so in a fit of despair, Henry drove to Godalming Ambulance Station at 4 am and banged on the door, only to find the crew were in darkness.

The men telephoned for a midwife and doctor, set up a generator and gave 19-year-old Jillian some valium to calm her down. She lay down on a mattress on the floor but said they had not the right equipment to deliver.

Later, under a dramatic police escort, she was rushed to St Luke's Hospital in Guildford, with blue lights flashing and sirens blaring. Little Thomas arrived at 11 am weighing 8lbs 4ozs. In hospital he was known as 'Hurricane Higgins' but the nurses said if he had been a girl, he would have been called Gail!

Not even the youngster's great-great-grandfather, who lived to the ripe old age of 106 would have known a storm like the one on October 16th 1987.

The Firemen Prayed

THE fire crew called out to Oaks Park will never know how they survived the night as 100 foot high trees crashed around them like "balsa wood". Their story exemplifies the many miracles of the night.

Shortly after midnight,Wallington Fire Station's "White Watch" were called out to clear a fallen tree from Woodmansterne Road. Barely able to make themselves heard against the noise of the gale, they yelled at each other as they drew up by the heavily wooded park. A policewoman already there, advised them to turn back.

As the winds picked up even more strength, trees started to splinter and crash down all around them. Station officer Arthur Hookway described the moments that followed as the most frightening of his life. The force of the wind was 'supernatural'.

Two youths who had abandoned their cars appeared and were persuaded to seek shelter aboard the fire engine. They had come from north London and were trapped in the mayhem of Oaks Park. Their cars were crushed minutes after they left them.

Station officer Hookway said the tree across the road was moved but they were now falling like ninepins. He told Croydon control he was moving his crew to safety and would find shelter for the rest of the night.

As the engine was being reversed, an enormous tree crashed down on the spot where it had been parked. Another thudded down 20 yards ahead and the crew realised that the wrong move would mean death or serious injury. They prayed, searched again for safety and found a small holding cottage.

The petrified crew and the two youths were given refuge for the rest of the night and one of them, fireman Chris Bartlett was able to call his wife who was expecting a baby and reassure her he was all right. In the dark, they sipped cups of tea.

Station officer Hookway said the Brixton riots and other disturbances were nothing to him compared with the events of that night. "We lived", he said, "by the luck of the draw".

His comment was supported by later statistics. In the woods alongside Woodmansterne Road 15,000 trees fell in the seven hours the firemen were on the scene.

Photograph: Mark Davison

Mention Oaks Park to these fire-fighters at Wallington and their blood turns cold!

Telecom Tale

AS the great storm subsided and the people of Surrey awoke from their uneasy slumbers, ventured forth from cellars and 'safe rooms' or stepped across the debris of their own home, there was a feeling of utter disbelief. The landscape looked like a victim of a nuclear holocaust. For those who were able to tune into car or battery radios the grimness of the situation was contained in a short, crisp message. 'Stop using your telephones', a newsflash warned. 'Make only essential calls. The whole system is about to collapse'.

Listeners to Radio Mercury heard these astonishing words which were repeated over and over again. Those overhead telephone lines which somehow had survived the night were sagging pathetically but people were still making calls. Staff at the overloaded exchanges thought the network would collapse completely.

No power, roads blocked by fallen trees, no water in many homes and now, no telephones. Surrey's brittle link with the outside world had completely died.

In British Telecom's South-London district, covering such places as Mitcham, Caterham, Redhill, Woldingham and in the 01 areas of Croydon, Balham and Beckenham, there were 16,000 line faults. From an early inspection it was clear it would take weeks, perhaps months, to restore the phones. Poles were smashed and the lines lay in a twisted, tangled coil under tons of debris. The task facing engineers was daunting but the men worked all daylight hours, seven days a week, often soaked to the skin to reduce the enormous backlog of faults.

Southern London's plea for help was answered by other districts and reinforcements poured into Surrey. Within a week 100 external engineers had arrived to back up the local workforce. They came from all over the country; two drove down from Dundee in BT vans, six came from Edinburgh, two from Truro, six from Liverpool and others from Birmingham, Bristol, Inverness, Swindon and the Solent district. In Surrey's most rural areas those men of mixed dialects worked together as an unusual but highly successful team.

Like the Seeboard engineers the men needed beds for the night and personnel manager, Terry Chapman, appealed for accommodation while welfare officer, Peter Hynes, took on the unusual role of emergency billeting officer. Staff from the personnel department manned the telephone in shifts in the welfare office of the Croydon Telephone Exchange.

As Surrey's telephone link was gradually restored, the South London district general manager spoke of his admiration for all the men who worked such long hours in appalling conditions. Many had their own storm damage problems at home but postponed personal needs in order to help others. Surrey will always be proud of these courageous men.

Photograph: British Telecom

British Telecom staff from different regions work together to restore power in Old Farleigh Road, Selsdon near Croydon. The local men are Stan Richardson and Gary Kirby from Coulsdon and Jeffrey Pike, Clive Rutter and Keith Walker from the Severnside District.

Guests from Brum

by Linda Brockey from British Telecom

TWO engineers sent down from Birmingham were working on restoring service to a large country house in Betchworth near Dorking when the lady of the house asked them how they were enjoying their spell in the south.

"Not too bad," they said. "But we don't go much on our digs."

Straight away, she offered to put them up in her summer house. Peter Grew and Doug Turland agreed at once, and a short time later, moved in.

They found the fridge ready stocked with beer for them. Tea, coffee and milk were laid on and the pair were told to use the family's swimming pool and sauna and tuck into a pheasant supper.

Like the other external engineers sent down to Southern London, Doug and Peter were working seven days a week. "We agreed to go down south on the Thursday after the storm, went into work on the Friday and were given two hours' notice to get packed and get going," they said. "We didn't even have a chance to say goodbye to our wives."

Graham Harrison from Derby, staying at a pub in Redhill, said he had quickly become friends with the local engineers he found himself working with. "They invited us home for meals in the evening, and Sunday lunch," he said.

One thing that came as a shock to all the visiting engineers was the price of beer and the price of property 'down south'.

"Most of us have never been here before," said one. "We're enjoying it and would volunteer again if ever the need arose, even if it is hard work. But we couldn't afford to live here!"

Photograph: Gordon Allis, Banstead Herald

Croydon Lane, Banstead, on the morning of October 16, 1987, hours after the widespread devastation of Oaks Park on the right.

Photograph: Ian Currie

The same area today after a long and costly operation.

Photograph: Keith Harding, Dorking

The hurricane-force winds screamed over Reigate Hill, felling hundreds of beech trees on the National Trust parkland. Some areas of woodland in the vicinity lost just one or two trees. Others lost 90 per cent, leading to speculation that the winds at this point probably exceeded 110 mph.

Story of a lifetime

THE nightmare of October 16 was an eerie reality for 100-year-old Mrs Annie Smith when suddenly in the early hours she was woken by a diabolical noise. As she sat up in bed and tried to regain her senses she became aware of a chill in the room. The windows were barely open but the curtains blew in the most extraordinary wind and the noise had escalated to a tremendous roar, like the sound of an express train travelling through a tunnel.

Faced with sleeplessness Mrs Smith bravely decided to get dressed. The curtains were blowing but she hadn't bargained for the wind that nearly blew her away. As she battled her way downstairs Mrs Smith thought she would rest her nerves and join her daughter Betty for a cup of tea but as soon as they put the kettle on, the lights went out.

The remainder of the night passed in darkness and terror for the two ladies. Like the rest of the south they could only guess at what was happening around them. In her 100 years, Mrs Smith said she had never known a storm of such ferocity.

Compared with some areas of the country the ladies escaped lightly, losing a few roof tiles and a tree that crashed in the garden. Over the road Mitcham Common lay almost bare, a skeleton, while the town was brought to a halt. The story was the same all over Surrey, but to the 100-year-old lady it was the story of a lifetime.

Photograph: Style Setters, Mitcham.

Annie Smith

The bus service in Surrey and South London was virtually non-existent on the day of the Great Storm. Crews were unable to get to work, and so many roads were blocked, the normal routes could not be taken where a bus was available for service. Here, at Streatham Common, a deserted bus shelter provided little refuge from the gale.

Photograph: Surrey and South London Newspapers

A Hard Day's Night

for a freelance photographer

THURSDAY night October 15, 1987 was like any evening for John Powell. He watched television, made himself a drink, and not paying too much attention, heard the late night news and weather, before retiring to bed.

There was no hint of any storm. In fact, the news was quite mild, he recalled. He drifted off to sleep, but in bed, in the dead of the night, his dog, Yogi, a German Shepherd, made sure he woke up. John stirred and realised the wind was unusually strong so he peered out of the window of his home in Danescourt Crescent, Sutton, and saw the trees blowing crazily in his garden, and the fence flattened.

John put it down to an autumnal gale and went back to sleep. In any case, it was so dark and black out there, he may have been imagining what he saw. Three hours later, his restless dog was still upset, so John took him for a walk in the park at Rose Hill.

He found trees lying on their sides in the murky light and the wind was blasting in tremendous gusts. John thought of his camera, but it was surely still too dark. He turned to see a tree right across the fence of Greenshawe High School, and another lying partly across the road.

John rushed back home, picked up his camera, and at 7am started a day's work that was to last until 2am the next morning.

His first job of the day was photographing a group of Hungarian ballet dancers at Wimbledon Theatre. The roads were littered with twigs and branches, but John managed to get to Wimbledon without fuss. He had been told that 200 children from Merton, Mitcham and Morden would be watching the show, but he was introduced to a small gathering of only four dozen youngsters. The other children were trapped by fallen trees in and around Merton.

The dancing display went ahead, but after taking a few shots, he was wanted urgently by the Wimbledon News and South London News office. 'Go to Wimbledon, Mitcham, Streatham and Balham and take as many pictures as possible of the storm damage,' he was told. John's first pictures were of trees which had fallen on a new housing estate off Church Lane next to Tooting Bec Hospital.

He found damaged bus shelters and crash barriers at Streatham Common and walls demolished in Balham Park Road. In Balham's main shopping street, trees lay across pavements, and rubbish lay strewn across the A24. It was here, that a traffic warden asked how long he would be. 'One hundredth of a second,' he replied.

There were trees across the pavement at Tooting Bec and at Wandsworth Common, a leafy giant, thought to be at least 100 years old had come down opposite The Surrey Tavern in Trinity Road, wrecking a large area of tall wire fencing and missing the pub by feet.

The intrepid photographer had no time to eat. Just a few hundred yards from The Surrey Tavern in Bellevue Road, lorries and cars were forced to squeeze round a large tree which had toppled over the highway. At Wimbledon Hill a family could not get out of their drive in The Causeway for fallen trees, so they all grabbed a saw and got to work — including the mother.

Photograph: Surrey and South London Newspapers

The building next to where this car was parked collapsed in the hurricane and Police had to seal off Credenhill Street, Streatham, because of the danger to the public. For this girl, it was a shattering experience to find this was all that remained of the 18th birthday present from her grandparents.

The wind blew out more than 1000 bricks from this derelict building in Credenhill Street between Streatham and Mitcham.

Photograph: Surrey and South London Newspapers

OY OY OY, what's going on here, then? This spot of trouble in the Balham Park Road area could be a job for the special branch!

Stripped of their titles, these thin poles stand as if in a firing range at Wonham Mill, Betchworth, near Dorking.

Comprehensive destruction at Monks Orchard Rd., Shirley.

Photograph: Wimbledon News

It was all hands to the log on Wimbledon Hill when trees crashed down, not just on the famous Common, but across the driveways of houses, blocking in cars. Here, a family in The Causeway, which overlooks the lawn tennis club, get their teeth into the wood.

Nightmare in Bankside Close

NORMALLY, Bankside Close, in Carshalton Beeches, is a quiet retreat of neat town houses away from the hustle and bustle of nearby Croydon and Sutton. Its houses, built about 17 years ago are set into a former quarry last used in the 1800's, and the steep sides had become thickly wooded.

It was around 2am when the residents realised that the night ahead was going to be one which they would never forget. The wind howled and shrieked and a tall sycamore tree crashed down wrecking a red Ford Escort. Its 18-year-old owner had just bought it.

Another tree hit number 9, damaging the side of the house and residents risked death or injury as they strove to move their cars at the height of the storm. Mr Ellis, of number 6, said that with every gust of wind they thought a tree was going to smash into their house and he quickly brought his children from their upstairs bedroom to a ground floor room.

The storm was causing havoc all over the borough of Sutton. Trees were being tossed aside as if an army of giants was on the rampage. With a sledgehammer blow, a fearsome squall sent a tree crashing down on to number 17 extensively damaging the side of the house. By now, the residents of Bankside Close were marooned as tree after tree piled up across their only access.

When daylight came, the scene was one of utter devastation. Outside was a mass of twisted timber, three wrecked cars, two badly damaged houses and trees across the gardens. It was as if an earthquake had struck in Surrey.

It took three days of continuous hard work with heavy lifting gear before Bankside residents were able to drive out of their little road, and 24 hours before it was safe to make the journey on foot. For some it was impossible to leave their home, so deep was the debris against their doors. The Fire Brigade checked to see if anyone was hurt or trapped. But miraculously, all was well.

In the huge rescue operation that followed, one scene will remain in people's minds for a long time. It is looking up and seeing a car dangling over the roof tops as it was plucked out of the cul-de-sac by a giant crane.

Photograph: Martin Ellis

Bankside Close after the storm where residents were marooned for several days.

Many of the famous Purley Beeches fell. With increasing suburbanisation each tree is sorely missed.

Naturalists fear the loss of ground flora in the destructive wholesale clearance of the fallen timber. Species such as the bluebell, wood anemone, dog mercury and many others may be severely reduced in number and it could take very many decades for them to re-appear. For this reason natural regeneration or very sensitive clearing only should be encouraged in order to keep the woodland floor intact.

Photograph: Dr William Latimer, Surrey Wildlife Trust

The Sheepleas. An example of clear felling where the delicate balance of the woodland floor has been totally destroyed.

Happy anniversary, storm!

HAPPY? — well yes, if you are concerned with wildlife conservation in Surrey. Certainly the damage was extensive — rough estimates indicate about 10 per cent of all trees in the county damaged in some degree — and many fine old trees were lost. Some areas of woodland have been completely devastated by the storm, and here one cannot say that wildlife benefits: it will be 50 years or more before the woodland community returns. Gardens, parks, and other areas where specimen trees have been lost also cannot recover.

But over most of the county the natural woodlands remain, and will be a much richer wildlife habitat in the future. Most of the damaged trees are recovering well, and where trees were blown over, or snapped off at the trunk and so can't recover, new tree seedlings are appearing.

Also, in these clearings, there is often an abundant show of wild flowers; and sun-loving insects, like butterflies, feed on their nectar. Other insects are feeding on the fallen timber, which is now beginning to decay — and they in their turn will be food for woodpeckers, tree-creepers, wrens, and other birds.

In the longer term, as the new seedlings grow, our woods will develop a much more varied structure of old and young trees — more attractive to look at, as well as better for wildlife.

Or at least they should — unless landowners, over-zealous for "clearing up", destroy them. There is a risk of far greater damage to woodlands now than resulted from the storm itself.

In many woods there is a good deal of timber blown over or so damaged that it must be harvested, and landowners are, quite reasonably, anxious to extract this before it loses value. But there are many different ways to do the job. Some landowners are using the storm damage as an excuse to clear totally large areas of woodland, lifting all the stumps, burning all the branchwood, and machine-levelling the site prior to replanting. This may well make future commercial management of the new plantation easier, but it has in the process destroyed the whole wildlife community. What had been a damaged, but recovering, semi-natural woodland is reduced to an artificially planted crop of little more value to wildlife than a field of wheat.

Timber can be extracted without such destruction. A little fore-thought and planning allows machinery to be confined to chosen haul-routes, minimising damage to the woodland soil and flowering plants; careful cutting and felling can avoid damage to self-sown seedlings and saplings which will form part of the next generation;

stumps and unwanted branchwood can be left for the insects, and replanting (with native trees) can be done in the shelter of the surviving older trees. It only needs a little care.

Woodland owners now need advice and help in management of their woods. There is a heightened awareness of the importance of woodlands to all of us, and there is grant-aid available to assist in woodland work. The storm has given us a once-in-a-lifetime opportunity to influence the future development of our woodlands, and create something even better for the future. But what do we really want? More fundamentally, what have we got at present? We don't actually know.

Surrey Wildlife Trust has embarked on a survey which will tell us exactly what the storm did to Surrey's woodlands, and what we have left, in terms of both the species and ages of trees. From this we can predict what would happen to our woodlands if they were left unmanaged, or if they were actively managed in different ways.

We can identify what timber resources are available now, and what will be available in the future (you can't expect owners to manage woods without a reasonable return). Then we can put forward ideas for management which will ensure a financial return for the owners (essential if the woods are to survive in the long term) and also enhance their wildlife interest, for everyone to enjoy.

Surrey Wildlife Trust

The Old School House,
School Lane,
Pirbright,
Near Woking, Surrey
Telephone: (0483) 797575

The storm has its brighter side. It has saved many hours' effort that might have been necessary over the next decade by felling trees to create glades artificially. It has also presented a valuable opportunity to study the natural process of succession and woodland regeneration. Here, members of the Surrey Wildlife Trust examine the roots of a fallen tree. On the right Liz Brown, the Trust's Storm Officer who is surveying tree populations and advising landowners.

Three crazy years

WITH the severe cold and spectacular blizzards of January and the hurricane-force winds of October, 1987 became the most memorable meteorological year Surrey has ever known.

Twice in that year the working day ground to a halt as nature showed that she still has total command over twentieth century man. Surrey commuters hardened to the vicissitudes of the road and rail systems and the capriciousness of the weather, had to succumb to forces beyond their control. Surrey's one million people were all affected by these exceptional conditions.

The year 1987 had been preceded by some unusual weather conditions and there were strong arguments that the weather had become more extreme in recent years. January 1985 was bitterly cold and on several days the temperature never rose above minus 5 deg C (23F) at Coulsdon and Caterham. At Warlingham there were nine days when the mercury remained below freezing. The autumn of 1985 was extremely dry but, in many parts of Surrey, November was the coldest since 1923.

February 1986 was the coldest this century behind the infamous 1947. At Camberley, 17 cm (nearly seven inches) of snow fell on the 6th and in some parts of the country the temperature never exceeded 3 deg C (38 F) all month. The cold weather continued as Coulsdon recorded the lowest maximum of the century for March — 1.5 deg C (29 f). In Redhill, April was the coldest since 1936.

Perhaps one of the most unusual months was September 1986 which had the combination of dry and sunny yet terribly cold weather. It was the coldest September on record at Reigate and on the 15th temperatures never rose much above 9 deg C (48 F) from Caterham to Guildford — about 9 deg C (16F) below average. October was actually warmer than September, a very rare event.

After two years of crazy weather the scene was set for the most momentous year of all. 1987 began deceptively mild, almost spring-like, with 11 deg C (52 F) recorded at Guildford. With temperatures below minus 30 deg C (minus 22 F) over Scandinavia and Russia, an intense cold wave moved across Europe bringing heavy snow. Temperatures in the south-east plunged to sub-zero.

On January 12, 1987, the mercury amazingly stayed below minus 9 dec C (16F) at Warlingham despite blue skies and continuous sunshine. In Surrey, it was the coldest day of the century and at night, Caterham froze solid at minus 14 deg C (just 7F).

On the night of the 12th it started snowing; a powdery snow more akin to that in Canada or Siberia. The temperature remained low — minus 10 deg C (14 F) — and that itself was extremely rare. The snow fell harder and harder reaching a depth of 39 cm (15 inches) at Warlingham on the 14th and 23 cm (nine inches) at Guildford.

There was widespread disruption but worse was to follow as gale-force winds from the north-east drove the fine crystalline snow into massive drifts. Like the rest of south-east England, Surrey became a white blur. Transport was brought to a halt, schools, shops and offices closed and still it continued to snow.

Massive cornices of ice four metres (13 feet) high overhung the A217 at Reigate Hill, and at East Molesey and Hampton Court the Thames began to freeze.

The thaw, when it came, was gradual and flooding limited. There was no rain to add to the melting snow but there were numerous burst pipes and some parts of Surrey actually had water shortages.

After a nondescript February, March provided a taste of things to come as 70mph winds wreaked havoc across Surrey. In one incident three men were crushed to death when a giant beech tree crashed down on their mini-bus at Lower Kingswood. The ambulance carrying the injured to hospital had its windscreen smashed by a falling branch at Epsom.

April was the warmest since 1961. At Morden the temperature reached 25 dec C (77 F) and 24 deg C at Camberley. June was cool and wet; at Reigate it was the dullest since 1949 and at Coulsdon the wettest since 1966. August was more normal but the lowest maximum temperature since 1954 was recorded at Sanderstead on the 27th of just 12 deg C (54 F).

September 1987 was an average and reasonable month and the beginning of October was also quite sunny. The people of Surrey were lulled into thinking that the weather was benign at last but what was to follow was unforgettable.

There was widespread flooding across the county. Pyrford had a total of 246 mms (nearly 10 inches) and Guildford more than three times its normal monthly rainfall. At Leatherhead the River Mole burst its banks and at Thorncroft Bridge the road was flooded.

At Brockham, there was a dramatic rescue when a car plunged into the Mole. The driver clambered out of the window and clung to a bridge as his car disappeared under the murky waters. Farmers moved cattle to higher ground and firemen were busy pumping out flooded properties. The village of Beare Green was badly affected and the railway line from Redhill to Tonbridge was closed by floodwater.

Accompanying the floods were winds that reached hurricane force. They blew in from the sea and . . . . but that is another story!

It looks like Siberia but, in fact, it's London Road, Reigate, on the morning of January 14, 1987 when a north-easterly gale brought blizzard conditions to southern England.

No pen could describe it, nor tongue express it, nor thought conceive it unless by one in the extremity of it.

Daniel Defoe on the Great Tempest of Nov 26, 1703

About the Authors

Mark Davison

WHEN Mark Davison is not at his office desk in Reigate where he is deputy editor of The Surrey Mirror Series he can usually be found studying the varied but unpredictable British climate.

As a journalist Mark has worked in Kingston and Redhill, enjoyed a brief sortie around the peaks of Derbyshire and returned to The Surrey Mirror with executive responsibilities.

As an amateur meteorologist he has studied Surrey's range of extreme conditons from snowstorms and fogs to protracted droughts, heatwaves, and hailstorms and has an amazing photographic collection representing each phenomenon.

Mark compiled and produced his newspaper's commemorative hurricane edition after returning from holiday in Corfu where, in a mountain-top taverna, he met the people stranded on the Surrey "ghost train". He 'phoned the story over and returned to the bar!

Ian Currie

IAN Currie has spent all his working life as a teacher of geography and meteorology. He is well known for his weekly weather column in the Surrey Mirror, Sutton Herald and Surrey Comet series of newspapers and is heard each week on Radio Redhill.

In 1974 Ian joined the Climatalogical Observers Link and operates a weather station at his home in Coulsdon. He is a Fellow of the Royal Meteorological Society and he has an Open University Degree based on geography and earth science.

Ian holds evening classes on weather studies, organises field courses and talks to local groups and societies. He re-established the meteorology section of the Croydon Natural History and Scientific Society in Croydon, and has acted as a consultant on meteorological matters to various local firms.

Ian is married with two boys who woke him up on the night of October 16, 1987 to alert him to Surrey's biggest weather event since 1703.

Ian Currie (left), Mark Davison (right)